In Stanley's Footsteps

Henry Morton Stanley (January, 1878).

In Stanley's Footsteps

Across Africa from West to East

John and Julie Batchelor

BLANDFORD

Blandford
An imprint of Cassell
Artillery House, Artillery Row
London SW1P 1RT

First published 1990

Distributed in the United States by
Sterling Publishing Co. Inc.
387 Park Avenue South, New York, NY 10016-8810

Distributed in Australia by
Capricorn Link (Australia) Pty Ltd
PO Box 665, Lane Cove, NSW 2066

British Library Cataloguing in Publication Data

Batchelor, John *1947–*
In Stanley's footsteps: across Africa from
west to east.
1. Africa.   Description & travel
I. Title   II. Batchelor, Julie
916′.04328

ISBN 0-7137-2116-2

Typeset by Asco Trade Typesetting Ltd, Hong Kong

Printed in Spain by Graficas Reunidas

Contents

To the memory of Helen

Acknowledgements

This book would not have been written without the aid of the many people who showed us unstinting hospitality and assistance along the rivers, trails and roads of Central Africa. To them all we say '*mbote*', '*jambo*', and thank you.

We acknowledge the generous support of Ethiopian Airlines and thank them for bringing us home with such efficiency and in such comfort. Our special thanks to Peter Talkington and David O'Sullivan at the London office for making it possible.

In researching the book we owe a great debt to the Royal Geographical Society and their comprehensive collection of Stanley material. Our thanks to the librarian, Mr David Wileman, and his staff, for their knowledgeable direction and help.

The photograph of Stanley on the front cover is from the Royal Geographical Society collection. All black-and-white illustrations are taken from contemporary sources.

Note

Our policy has been, when writing in the historical context, to apply names and the spelling of names as used by Stanley and his officers, whilst adhering to modern-day names and spellings in the account of our own journey.

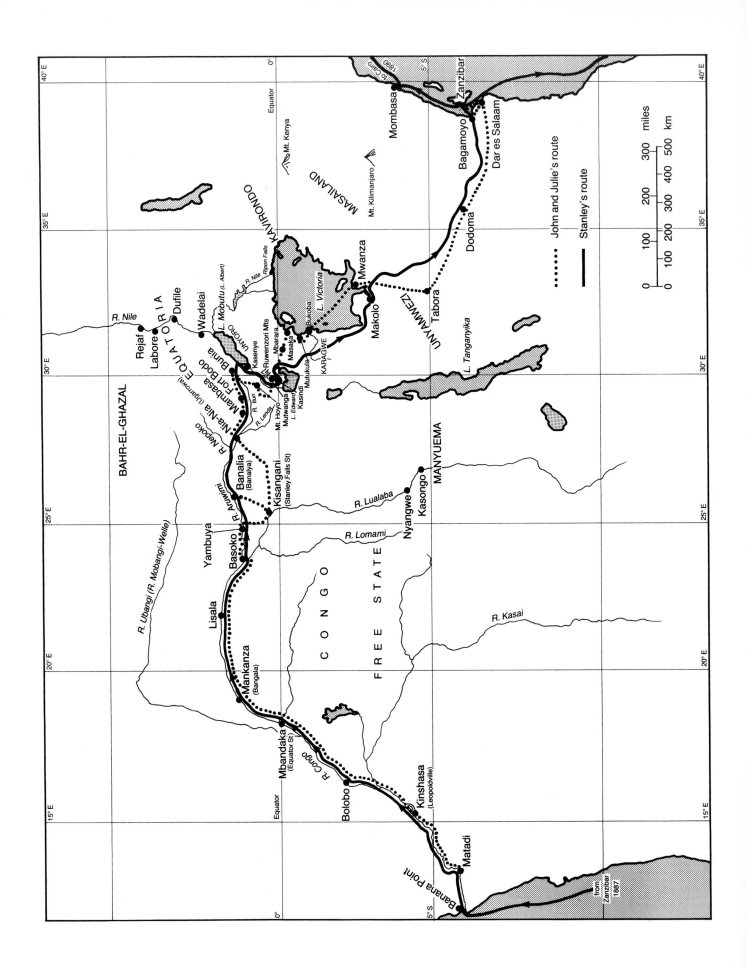

Back to Africa

The crowd pressed forward, eager to catch a glimpse of the famous faces beyond the barrier. The stocky figure of the explorer separated itself from the group on the platform, boarded the train, then turned to acknowledge the crowd's cheers. The whistle blew and the continental mail train pulled slowly out of Charing Cross Station. Settling back in his seat, Henry Morton Stanley closed his eyes for a moment of private contemplation. The hectic weeks of preparation were over, his last African adventure had begun. His task, to rescue a man named Emin Pasha from the heart of Africa.

On that evening of 21 January 1887 he was just seven days away from his forty-sixth birthday. He had much to reflect on, much to be thankful for. Born John Rowlands, the illegitimate son of a Welsh housemaid, he had come a long way in the world. Who would have thought that the waif abandoned to the tender mercies of the St Asaph workhouse would become the confidant of kings and carve a position for himself as the foremost explorer of his day? Escape to America at the age of 15 years had set the wheels in motion. In the house of a wealthy cotton broker in New Orleans he had found a new family, a new name and for a time the security of a home life that he had never known before. Store-keeping might have become his life's work had it not

been for the advent of the American Civil War. He was swept into the conflict, starting out on the Confederate side and ending up with the Union troops. After the war he knocked around for a few years, briefly returning to North Wales, making an eventful journey with friends to Asia Minor and eventually falling into a job as a journalist back in America.

His coverage of the Indian Wars brought Stanley to the attention of the man who was to propel him to fame, James Gordon Bennett, publisher of the *New York Herald*. Bennett sent him to Abyssinia to report on the British invasion under Sir Robert Napier. Showing ruthless single-mindedness he scooped the story of the British victory by the simple expedient of bribing the telegraph operator to send only his report. This coup set him on the road to fame and fortune.

Bennett was impressed with his new reporter and rewarded him with a roving commission and a long list of assignments, the last of which was 'to find David Livingstone', the missionary explorer who had disappeared into the vast expanses of Central Africa. In November 1871 at Ujiji on the shores of Lake Tanganyika the famous meeting took place between the doctor and the journalist. This adventure was to change Stanley's life. The amateur traveller had succeeded

H.M. Stanley, from a portrait by F. Moscheles.

where professionals had failed. He had discovered a natural talent for expedition organisation and a love of Africa. The blaze of publicity that greeted him on his return to Europe soon convinced Stanley that it was better to be the subject of attention rather than the reporter of others' deeds.

By 1874 he was back in Africa to make his epic 999-day crossing of the continent from the Indian Ocean to the Atlantic. The reporter had become an explorer, but that was not enough. Now he was to be the founding father of a nation. Returning to the Congo in 1879 he spent five years on the mammoth task of creating the Congo Free State for his patron, King Leopold II of the Belgians. Back in Europe in 1884 he filled his time writing his third best-selling book and starring on the international lecture circuit. All this might certainly seem a life full enough for any man in his forties, but it was not enough to satisfy the restless spirit of the explorer. He cast around for some more testing and demanding assignment.

When the call came he was in America at the start of a lecture tour. The cancellation of that commitment alone cost him £10,000 in lost fees, and that took no account of the 139 lectures booked to follow in Australia. But money and lecture theatres held little attraction when the opportunity to mount the rostrum of world affairs came his way and he could once again stand at the centre, his words awaited by the largest audience of all. He had taken up the challenge, had sought it, now he must follow it through and perform for a demanding public. As the train rushed on through the night bearing Stanley towards his latest appointment with destiny, the brief moment of reflection was over. Now was the time for action. Doubts must be put aside. He would succeed, he would survive to tell the tale.

*****

A hundred years later John and I were making plans to follow Stanley back to Africa. We had visited the continent many times before, but the thrill of

13

anticipation is never lost, the experience always new and unpredictable. To us these are essential ingredients of living. The centenary provided us with an excellent excuse for a journey, a rationalisation of the desire to answer the call that Africa has over its own. William Hoffman, Stanley's servant who accompanied him on the expedition, knew the feeling: 'Africa, once it has been visited, creeps insidiously into the traveller's blood and calls him back into its depths with an uncanny fascination.'

Our objective was to retrace the route of Stanley's expedition as closely as was possible for two lone travellers with limited resources. The journey we were preparing to follow was the Emin Pasha Relief Expedition.

*****

Few today will know the name of Emin Pasha, but during the late 1880s and early 1890s his was the story that filled the newspapers and periodicals. He was governor of Equatoria, the most southerly province of Sudan occupying a strip of land along the Nile where modern-day Sudan, Zaïre and Uganda meet. Now an independent country, Sudan was then ruled by Egypt. In 1883 its capital, Khartoum, fell to the forces of the Mahdi, General Gordon was killed, the British relief troops were defeated and the Sudan was abandoned. All was lost except for Equatoria, where Emin still held out. For the newspapers of the day the province represented the last outpost against the advancing armies of evil. Gordon was lost, the same fate must not be allowed to befall Emin.

Little was known of this mysterious figure who, despite his name, was thought to be a European. He was in fact German, his real name Eduard Schnitzer. It was not unusual in the Sudan at that time to find men who wished to lose their identities and make new lives for themselves. In Schnitzer's case he was running away from complicated domestic problems. He had for most of his adult life

Sir W. Mackinnon, Chairman of the Emin Pasha Relief Committee and President of the British East Africa Company.

worked as a doctor in various corners of the Ottoman Empire and had adopted the life style of a Turk. But none of this was known to the public. The cry was to save this last standard-bearer of civilisation. The British government declined to become directly involved after their earlier failures, but they did give encouragement to private enterprise to take up the cause.

The call was quickly answered and by the autumn of 1886 the Emin Pasha Relief Committee had been formed. It was chaired by William Mackinnon (later Sir William), a shipping magnate soon to head the Imperial British East Africa Company (IBEAC), and staffed by his business associates and other notables. The committee had little difficulty in financing the expedition. About half the initial £21,500 came from the Egyptian government, whose nominal responsibility Equatoria was. The rest was raised by public subscription, or more accurately from just 17 subscribers consisting of Sir William and his close associates. Apart from Stanley there were a number of well-qualified candidates keen to lead the expedition, but once his interest was known there was little chance of the task being given to anyone else. He was already personally known to Mackinnon and was in any case the most experienced and trustworthy contender. There was one small problem. Although Stanley had not worked for King Leopold for two years, he was still retained by the King in connection with his Congo Free State enterprise. Leopold was never slow to grasp

Colonel Sir Francis de Winton, Secretary of the Relief Committee and, later, Administrator of British East Africa.

any advantage he could for his Congo empire and in this expedition he could certainly see benefits. He gave permission for the release of Stanley on one main condition, that the expedition should travel by way of the Congo River. As an incentive he was prepared to make available his Congo River 'flotilla' as transport. From the King's point of view, he would have an unknown corner of the Congo explored at little cost and would have improved his political position should there be a way of annexing Equatoria for his own ends.

There had been much debate about the route that Stanley should take. The most obvious, and best established, was that from the East Coast. Prior to Leopold's intervention, in fact, one of the East Coast caravan routes had been decided on, but now all that changed. After a private meeting between the King and Mackinnon, who had many business interests in common, there was no further argument. Just 13 days before departure it was agreed that the largely unknown Congo route should be followed.

So all was set. Stanley was recalled from America and in the incredibly short period of four weeks the expedition was under way. The thousand and one preparations had been made, Stanley's travelling companions had been chosen from the hundreds of men who had begged to go, and they had been sent on ahead.

Stanley had never ventured into Africa without the help of Zanzibari porters, and this latest expedition was to be no exception. At Zanzibar it was planned to take on board 600 porters and most of the provisions and trade goods that would be needed. But Stanley's first port of call was Egypt, where he arrived on 27 January 1887. His main tasks were to convince the Khedive and his government that the Congo route was feasible, which he did, then to arrange for the shipment of the munitions and a detachment of Sudanese soldiers supplied by the Egyptians, and lastly to receive written instructions for Emin from his employers.

Whilst in Cairo he also solved the last of his staffing problems, signing on Surgeon T H Parke as expedition doctor.

Having completed his business in Cairo in a week, Stanley sailed for Aden where he was to join up with the majority of his officers for the trip to Zanzibar. The ten-day cruise aboard the *Oriental* gave Stanley and his men their first opportunity to get to know one another. On this pressure-free leg they all seem to have got along well enough. The characters who were to play their parts in the unfolding drama of the Emin Pasha Relief Expedition were a motley collection of professional soldiers and gentlemen adventurers: Major Edmund Barttelot of the Seventh Fusileers, 26 years old, had served in India and the Sudan and was second-in-command to Stanley; Captain R H Nelson of Methuen's Horse had served in the Zulu campaigns in South Africa; Lieutenant W G Stairs, 24-year-old officer of the Royal Engineers; Surgeon T H Parke, who had served in Sudan, was 30 years old, a friend of Barttelot, and expedition doctor; William Bonny, ex-sergeant in the Army Medical Department, 40 years old, was medical assistant to the expedition; Mr A J Mounteney Jephson, 29 years old, a gentleman of no relevant experience, qualified by the contribution of £1000 and his travelling expenses; James S Jameson, 31 years old, a member of the famous Irish whiskey family, widely travelled on big-game hunting and sketching safaris, also contributed £1000 plus expenses and was the expedition naturalist; finally, there was William Hoffman, just 20 years old, Stanley's personal servant who was to accompany his master throughout the expedition. Of the hundreds of men who applied to join the expedition, it is difficult to conclude that this was the best qualified or, more importantly, the most

In 1887 Stanley and the expedition visited Zanzibar to take on men and supplies before sailing for the Congo. The Sultan's 'Palace of Wonder' on the water front had just been built.

compatible team that could be found. However, these were the men whom Stanley had personally selected to accompany him, and if all did not turn out as expected or desired, the responsibility would have to rest with the leader.

The expedition spent three hectic days on the island of Zanzibar, organising the loading of men and materials on to the ship which was to take them to the Congo. Stanley left his officers to deal with this task while he saw to 'several little commissions' unrelated to expedition affairs. Firstly, he negotiated a small piece of business on behalf of Sir William Mackinnon with the elderly Sultan of Zanzibar, Seyyid Barghash. The Sultan was ruler not only of Zanzibar and Oman, but also of the whole of East Africa from the Indian Ocean to the Congo River. Suzerainty had been established over the centuries by virtue of the fact that Zanzibar was the main trading centre

and sponsor of the armed Arab caravans that penetrated deep into the interior in search of ivory and slaves. This authority was now being eroded by the European powers, firstly by the arbitrary carving up of Africa at the Berlin Conference of 1884 and secondly by the Anglo–German agreement of 1886 which defined the two parties' relative 'spheres of influence' in East Africa. The Germans had already established themselves on the mainland and were taking control of an area which was to become the German East African colony. Now it was Stanley's job to procure a foothold in East Africa for British free enterprise. With surprising ease, the Sultan agreed to grant Sir William a trading agreement covering an area roughly equivalent to the coastline of modern-day Kenya. This concession would become the initial area of operation for the IBEAC and form the basis for eventual expansion into the British colonies of Kenya and Uganda. Sir William's investment in the Emin Pasha Relief Expedition had already paid handsome dividends.

The second matter to be attended to was for Stanley's other patron, King Leopold of the Belgians. This brings into the spotlight one of the most interesting players in the drama of Central African politics, the Arab trader Hamed bin Muhammed el Murjebi, more commonly known as Tippu Tip. This man had carved out for himself a vast empire encompassing the whole of the eastern Congo and large parts of the south extending to Katanga. He was a man of dark negroid appearance, being of mixed Bantu and Arab blood, who claimed his mother was an African princess. At the time of this meeting with Stanley he was about 45 years old. The explorer was well known to Tippu as they had met during Stanley's first crossing of Africa when the Arab trader had assisted him on his journey down the Congo River, a service for which Tippu always claimed he was still awaiting full payment.

Stanley now set before him a proposal from King Leopold. In essence it offered

Tippu the position of Governor of the Stanley Falls station at a salary of £30 per month, in return for which he would raise the Congo Free State flag in all the areas that he controlled and would agree to suppress the slave trade. In the first place this offered Tippu nothing he did not already have and in the second it seemed highly unlikely that he would wish to do anything to suppress the trade that formed the basis of his wealth. The background to this offer was that in Tippu's absence in Zanzibar from his settlement at Stanley Falls, at the head of navigation on the Congo River, the Arabs there had thrown out the Free State representative, an Englishman named Deane, which meant that Leopold's control now extended no further than the

Tippu Tip, infamous ivory and slave trader and Governor of Stanley Falls.

18

Zanzibar Town seen from the sea. It was from this bay that the expedition set sail for the Congo in the SS Madura *on 25 February 1887.*

river station of Bangala, some 500 miles west of Stanley Falls. The advantages for the King were obvious. He would re-establish a presence at the Falls station and, at least nominally, gain sovereignty over the whole of the area controlled by Tippu Tip. Tippu, a shrewd man, had already recognised that the Europeans were the coming force and that it was only a matter of time before he would have to step aside. His view was that he should make the best deal he could whilst the opportunity still existed. However, he ruled under the authority of the Sultan of Zanzibar and needed his consent before agreeing to any deal. The only point that seemed to worry Tippu was the insultingly small fee. Here is his account of his meeting with the Sultan:

I took it to Seyyid and told him what had passed. Seyyid advised me to go, and to go as far as they wanted. I complained to him about the wage they were giving me, thirty pounds a month. But he maintained I should go even for ten pounds a month, and I would still be able to carry on my business.

It is clear from this that only lip service was to be paid to the clause on the suppression of the slave trade.

Having succeeded in this mission, Stanley turned his attention to expedition business and the other service required of Tippu. He would be taking too few porters with him to carry all the goods provided for the relief of Emin Pasha, so an agreement was struck whereby Tippu would supply the extra 600 men needed. At this stage it was thought that Emin held a large store of ivory. Relieving him of responsibility for this was seen as an excellent way not only of paying the expenses of the expedition, but also of turning a good profit. The plan was that Tippu Tip's porters would carry the relief goods to Emin and then return loaded with ivory to be sold through Tippu's good offices. This also was agreed. The infamous slave trader had now become a respected officer of the Congo Free State and a key member of the Emin Pasha Relief Expedition. All was ready. Tippu Tip and his retinue of 100 followers were the last group to go aboard the SS *Madura*. The porters hired in Zanzibar had been paid a four-month advance and immediately taken out to the ship. The *Madura* had moved well out from shore in order to avoid desertions, a regular problem for unwary explorers. Amongst the Zanzibaris was a group known as 'bounty men' whose objective was to sign on, receive their advance and then abscond. As the ship set sail for the far west coast of Africa, there must have been more than a few men on board who had expected to be at home in bed that night, richer by four months' pay.

The SS *Madura* sailed on the morning of 25 February 1887. The roll call of the expedition now numbered 806:

623 Zanzibari porters and headmen,
97 Arabs—Tippu Tip and his followers,
62 Sudanese—soldiers supplied by the Egyptians,
12 Somalis—hired by Barttelot at Aden,
9 Europeans,
2 Interpreters,
1 Gunboy—Baruti, Stanley's native servant.

The Zanzibaris and Sudanese were packed together in a hold below decks. Trouble was not long in coming. Within two hours of sailing, fierce fighting broke out between the two groups. The officers had a hard time separating the warring factions, but Stanley seemed pleased with this first opportunity to see them in action: 'After we had wiped the blood and perspiration away I complimented the officers, especially Jephson, Nelson and Bonny, for their share in the fray. They had behaved most gallantly.' In the months to come, the officers were to find that compliments from Stanley were rare indulgences.

Judging from the casualty list, it must have been quite an impressive battle whilst it lasted. 'The result of the scrimmage is ten broken arms, 15 serious gashes with spears on the face and head, and contusions on shoulders and backs not

worth remarking, and several abrasions of the lower limbs.'

*****

There was no overcrowding, and certainly no fighting, on our journey from Europe to Zaïre. The Air Zaïre DC10 deposited its small band of 50 passengers in Kinshasa after a flight lasting a mere six hours. It took Stanley and his officers three months to reach the same point.

I clutched John's arm as we emerged from the clouds on the approach to N'Djili Airport.

'Look, we're nearly there. You can see the river.' The silver ribbon of the Zaïre glittered below us. We could see its wooded islands and the massy forest on its banks. The familiar warmth and smells of the tropics wrapped themselves around us as we stepped from the plane. We were back in Africa.

If there was going to be any fighting it would be in the terminal building. We steeled ourselves for the assault of the expediters whose function is to process arriving passengers through customs and immigration. These expediters are freelances who pick up a few dollars for their services and generally succeed in spreading panic and confusion among their victims. There is no way of avoiding them. It is best just to flow with the stream. One man pushed his way towards us, beaming a broad, toothy smile. 'Passports, please!'

We handed them over and followed along. In reality the expediters are quite helpful, but their abrupt disappearance with one's passport can be disconcerting if you do not know the system. In front of us a large middle-aged American broke into a run, shouting at the top of his voice, 'Hi, that guy's stolen my passport!' By the time we reached the passport window the American seemed to have recovered his documents whilst his 'helper' was diligently trying to extract his medical certificates from his wallet for the next stage. This action seemed to have led to further misunderstanding. We caught up with our man at the end of the line and moved on to the Customs hall to await our luggage. A dozen porters, official this time, dressed in yellow overalls with numbers across the back, positioned themselves around each passenger, waiting to grab the baggage. As it started to appear our expediter and porters pressed forward.

'This your bag?' they shouted each time.
'No? What colour's yours?'
'It's blue.'
'Right, blue.' As each blue bag appeared there was a rush and a shout.
'This one?'
'No. Not that one.'

The excitement subsided until the next blue one arrived. This time it was ours. There was general disappointment when they saw we were rucksack types. But six men still managed to get a hand somewhere on each of our two bags and made to set off with them. Now was the time to show some authority. Stepping amongst the porters, John wrenched the bags physically from their grasp, and in his most commanding voice settled the matter.

'OK, two men only! I'll have numbers 26 and 130. You two carry the bags.'

The others started to complain vociferously.

'But I got hold of the bag first!'
'You can all carry the bags if you want, but only these two men will be paid.'

With that the losers drifted away.

We moved towards the customs bench, our assistant still in attendance. Now another job applicant crept up and whispered urgently in John's ear.

'You want a taxi, sir?'
'No!'

He smiled happily and stayed, sure he'd got the job. The customs men showed no interest in our baggage so our expediter was dispatched to get some attention. In due course an officer sauntered over, took one look at our rucksacks and without a word slashed a chalk mark across each. We were on our way.

Outside the touts without sufficient influence to get into the 'secure area' were clamouring to pick up a few crumbs of business. Our party of six forced a way through. More drivers appeared. 'Taxi, sir?' We did need a taxi so some decision had to be made.

'Has your taxi got a meter?' John asked the first driver.

'Oh yes, very nice meter.'
'OK, let's go.'

Our little caravan marched out into the car park and came to a halt next to a battered yellow saloon of no discernible make. There was no sign of a meter.

'All right, where's the meter?' John demanded.

'Oh, no meter, but give good price,' the driver said as he secured the boot with a long piece of rope.

'How much?'
'Fifty dollars.'

More drivers could be seen approaching at a run. It was in everyone's interest to finalise negotiations. We settled on 25 dollars. John paid off the porters and the expediter who all bitterly criticised the poverty of their tips. We scrambled into the car, but unfortunately, as there was no glass in the window, John was still under attack from our discontented ex-staff. Eventually the car lumbered forward and we seemed to have escaped our pursuers. But we did not get far. A hundred yards further on we were stopped by a barrier across the road, a police checkpoint. This was something we had not seen at the airport before but it could only be there for one reason, extortion. Sure enough, a policeman poked a smiling face inside the car.

'Twenty dollars road tax, sir.'

After a little debate we were allowed the freedom of the roads for the bargain price of five dollars. The taxi crawled forward, slowly gathering pace. At last we left the airport and joined the morning rush-hour traffic into Kinshasa, trundling along at a stately 15 miles per hour.

*****

After the battle below decks the rest of Stanley's sea voyage passed uneventfully. The *Madura* called in at Cape Town

21

briefly for fuel and to pick up another member of the party, an engineer named Walker whose job would be to get Leopold's boats up the Congo to the Aruwimi River. Once that task was completed he would be released from service. At the Cape, Tippu Tip and his people were objects of interest to the local whites who came aboard to inspect the famous slave trader.

Tippu was not the only person under inspection and assessment at that time. Stanley took the opportunity to note his thoughts on his officers in a letter to a friend:

Barttelot is a little too eager, and will have to be restrained. There is abundance of work in him, and this quality would be most lovely if it were always according to orders . . . There is a great deal in Mounteney Jephson, though he was supposed to be effeminate. He is actually fierce when roused, and his face becomes dangerously set and fixed. . . . He will either be made or marred if he is with this Expedition long enough.

Captain Nelson is a fine fellow, and without the ghost of a hobby: he is the same all round, and at all hours.

Stairs is a splendid fellow, painstaking, ready, thoughtful, and industrious, and is a valuable addition to our staff. Jameson is still the nice fellow we saw; there is not an atom of change in him. He is sociable and good.

Bonny is the soldier. He is not initiative. He seems to have been under a martinet's drill.

The muddy brown waters of the Congo River estuary meet the sea five degrees south of the equator and bear witness to the river's great size and power by gouging a huge canyon in the sea bed which extends far out into the Atlantic. The brown stain of Africa advances more than 300 miles before being overwhelmed by the ocean. There is no doubt that this is a major waterway, the seventh longest in the world and second only to the Amazon in volume of water poured into the sea.

On 18 March 1887 the expedition crossed the murky mass of silt and floating vegetation that had already made its journey from the very heart of Africa and hove to off Banana Point on the north bank of the river to await disembarkation. Their next step would be Matadi, 80 miles upstream, and from there would start the long road that they hoped was to lead to Emin Pasha and the relief of Equatoria.

*****

Kinshasa is the capital of Zaïre, one of the largest cities in black Africa, with a population of some three millions, a figure that is hard to believe if you see only the spacious, and often deserted, business centre of town. Life goes on not at the centre, but rather in the numerous suburbs, the 'cités', that ring the capital. It is a well-ordered and attractive place with little evidence of the poverty and shanty towns that are to be seen around many another African city. Certainly there was no evidence of any hardship amongst our fellow guests at the Inter-Continental Hotel. It was not a place in which we could normally afford to stay, but the management had generously offered us a few days as their guests to prepare for the journey.

Agnes M'bu, the super-efficient hotel PR officer, took us in hand and soon had us flying around town trying to pin down permit requirements for travelling up-country and the departure date of the elusive river boat we hoped would take us the 900 miles up the Zaïre to the Aruwimi River. At the *Ministère de Territoires* we were told that we would need a special permit and a guide to accompany us, but that first we should go to the *Ministère des Affaires Etrangères* to get copies of the telexes mentioned in our letter of introduction from the ambassador in London. Taking a guide sounded like a bad and expensive move, so we dropped the permit idea. In any case, trying to recover copies of the telexes was likely to be a lifetime's work. We would just press on and deal with any problems as they arose.

Kinshasa, capital of Zaïre, a busy modern city.

The first of these was the boat, which appeared to be lost somewhere in the mists of the upper river. No one could say for sure when, or if, it would turn up. The best information we had was that it might go next Monday, that the only way to get a ticket was to turn up personally on the day before sailing to pay for it, and that the boat was fully booked anyway. We were not too dismayed by this last piece of information as everything is always fully booked when cash payments are involved. It took us two days to arrive at that point. It was now Wednesday. Things seemed to be working out nicely. That should just allow us time to visit Matadi and be back in time for the boat.

As Matadi had been the jumping-off point for Stanley's journey, we wanted to start our crossing of Africa there, too. At the station the booking clerk was reluctant to let us have tickets for Thursday's train, insisting that the Friday express would be better. He finally gave in, sold us tickets and told us to be at the station at 6.30 am.

This was our last night of luxury at the Inter-Continental. Every time we returned to the room we found some little goodies had been left for us, a bottle of wine, canapés, chocolates or fruit. In the hotel's expensive restaurants we felt rather out of place amongst the sharply-dressed businessmen and aid officials who formed the clientele. It was a sad thought that the next time we were in Kinshasa we would have to pay our own way.

23

Tentative Steps

Kinshasa Central Station at 6 o'clock in the morning did not encourage optimism. There were no platforms that we could see. We came out of the station building straight into a network of sidings, where decrepit rolling stock stood rusting to the tracks. Cornering a man in uniform, I enquired if the Matadi train was in.

'Yes, that's it over there,' he said, indicating what we had taken to be a cattle train. In fact, most of it consisted of box cars with wrenched-off doors and floors strewn with withered grass. Nearer the front were three or four sections that might once have been described as carriages. Almost all the doors and windows were missing and only a few bare wooden seats remained inside. We clambered aboard. The dust was so thick that our footprints could be clearly seen as we made our way down the carriage.

'Well, at least we have seats,' I remarked, brushing off the worst of the grime.

'Yes, it should be an Interesting Experience,' John replied, using that expression beloved of the intrepid traveller who knows he is in for a bad time.

We sat silently for a while, contemplating the coming journey. The seats were already beginning to feel uncomfortably hard. 'Can you hear something?' I asked. 'It sounds as though the natives are on the warpath.' Sure enough, a steady chanting could be heard in the distance, slowly growing louder, a throbbing rhythm like a battle cry issuing from hundreds of throats. Approaching the station at a snail's pace was a train festooned with bodies. People hung out of windows and doorways, were suspended from the sides of the carriages and perched on the engine, while on the roof dozens of athletic young men were actually dancing. The chanting reached a roaring climax. As the train slowed to a halt hundreds of people dropped from it and began to run towards the station building. The chant became ragged and finally died. We had witnessed rush hour at Kinshasa Central.

After an hour we got under way with a bone-crunching jolt and proceeded to crawl around the town at a slower pace than people walking beside the track. After 20 minutes of this, John, who was standing in the doorway, came hurrying back to his seat. 'Brace yourself. We're under attack,' he said, gripping the seat as though it were about to be torn from him. We were pulling into a small halt, where nothing could be seen but a heaving mass of humanity. The young men in the vanguard had already hit us, invading the train in waves, racing to grab any available seats. The train juddered to a stop. The outside world disappeared from view as squirming bodies pressed around us. A woman clawed her way in through the window and scrambled over

The Kinshasa/Matadi railway was opened in 1898 to link the port and the capital, by-passing the 220 miles of rapids that block the lower reaches of the Zaïre River.

us. Bedlam reigned as people screamed and shoved and babies howled. But out of the chaos some sort of order began to emerge as everyone found their own small space. Now the journey had really begun.

The train shambled on, picking up more passengers at each stop. Like liquid finding a level, new arrivals slotted themselves into spaces that hadn't seemed to exist before. The influx of passengers had signalled the arrival of the travelling salesmen, who steadily ploughed a furrow up and down the length of the train. Some shouted their wares, some sang impromptu verses, others embarked on animated stories to capture the attention of their audience. Their wares were as varied as their patter—combs, mirrors, lotions and soaps, comics and religious

books, knickers slung by one leg from a long pole, kebabs in hot chilli sauce, and multi-coloured pills in long plastic strips carried round the vendor's neck like a scarf. At first the pill man did the best business. Customers chose the colour that took their fancy—it didn't seem to matter what the pills were—then the vendor would snip off the number of packets required. As the day wore on, however, the knicker man came into his own. To the mothers of the numerous babies on board, with no toilet facilities and nappies an unknown commodity, a dry pair of pants came as something of a relief. It was not only the babies who suffered discomfort. On a journey of over ten hours, with the crush making it almost impossible to leave our seats and the train never stopping long enough at a station for us to

25

rush for the bush, it was torment for us as well.

I was too preoccupied with the agony of the experience to remember much of the passing scenery. It seems to me now a blur of burnt grass hills with few trees. I only really started to take note of the countryside when it began to signal the approach of journey's end. By then the crowds had thinned a little and it was possible to stand by an open door and watch our progress along the sides of a deep wooded valley with a silver river tumbling over rocks below. At last, as the sun dipped to the horizon, we caught our first glimpse of the Zaïre River, a sheet of tortured, eddying water framed for a moment between dark rock hills. But by this time we had little interest in the beauty of the scene. All we wanted to see were the tangled lines and parked wagons that would mark our arrival at Matadi and the end of that painful journey. After ten hours—spent covering a mere 220 miles—it was an enormous relief to leave the purgatory of our wooden seat and the smell of those tightly packed bodies. It had indeed proved to be the Interesting Experience John had predicted.

Outside the station we stood in the forecourt deciding on our next move. Matadi is a town of steep cobbled streets where walking is a major physical exercise. We had hoped to find a taxi to take us up to the hotel, but as, inevitably, there were none in sight, we set off uphill on foot. The town is quite small and it was not long before we came breathlessly in sight of the Metropole Hotel, a striking and surprising building to find in a corner of Central Africa. Standing six storeys high, it is a replica of a Moorish palace, with a central open courtyard in which ancient creepers cling to the walls on their long journey towards the light. At reception we were relieved to find there was no problem in getting a room. In fact the place appeared to be quite empty.

'Did you have a good journey?' enquired the receptionist politely as he completed the formalities.

'We came by train,' I informed him.

'Ah,' he nodded understandingly. 'It is much better to come by road. A pity you were not warned in Kinshasa.'

'We were, but we thought it would be an interesting experience by train.'

'You Europeans have some strange ideas about what's interesting,' he said with a laugh.

We had to agree with him.

Our visit to Matadi was to be a short one as we had to be back in Kinshasa by Saturday evening to make arrangements to travel on the river boat. As it was now Thursday evening, that gave us only one full day to look around, so after a quick supper it was early to bed in preparation for the next day's activities.

Our first task next morning was to change a traveller's cheque. After wandering around the bank for a while we eventually located the foreign exchange facilities up a flight of unmarked steps at the back of the building. Here sat three men reading newspapers. 'Good morning. I'd like to change a US dollar traveller's cheque,' John announced. One of the men reluctantly put down his newspaper and slowly made his way to the counter. John handed him the cheque. He looked at it with interest for some time then asked, 'American dollars?'

'Yes, that's right.'

'Sorry, we don't have any American dollars.'

'No, I don't want dollars. I want to change it for zaïres.'

'You want to change it for zaïres?' he repeated in disbelief.

'Yes, that's right.'

'Well, I suppose that might be possible,' he said doubtfully.

Picking up the cheque, he took it gingerly to the desk where his two colleagues were sitting and a whispered conversation ensued. The cheque was passed from one to the other; they studied it, nodded, clicked their teeth and then seemed to come to a decision. Yes, something had definitely been decided. The man came over to us. 'I will have to ask the manager about this.' With that he disappeared through a door at the back of the office and we sat down to wait. This was clearly not going to be the simple operation we had envisaged. Twenty minutes later he reappeared bearing a sheaf of papers. 'The manager says we can change the cheque,' he informed us with a sigh. It was all such a burden.

Over the next half-hour three forms were filled out, a three-month-old list of exchange rates was extracted from a file, and we were ready to move to the next stage. The second clerk very slowly checked all the calculations on an ancient hand-cranked adding machine, stamped and signed the forms and passed them on to the third member of the trio. He in turn went through the whole operation again, adding his own set of stamps and signing off with a flourish. We were now handed four different pieces of coloured paper, all covered in a multitude of stamps and calculations, and told to take them downstairs to receive our money. We had been there an hour and there was still no sign of any cash. Back in the main banking hall downstairs a large crowd had gathered. In corners customers were busy counting heaps of dirty notes and packing them into suitcases. We joined one of the queues and eventually handed over our sheaf of papers, receiving in return a numbered disc. Now we had to wait for our number to be called by the teller who would give us our money. At last we approached the glass cage, stacked waist-high with bundles of notes. The teller selected a couple of slabs of money and handed them over. We had only changed 100 dollars but had ended up with over 200 notes in zaïres. Carrying a substantial amount of money in Zaïre is a real problem.

Outside the bank the day was already hot. We had wasted two hours in changing one traveller's cheque and most of the morning. As time was limited, we decided to hire a taxi for a few hours, our main aim being to cross to the far bank of the river to visit sites associated with Stanley. A taxi stopped and we explained to the driver what we wanted to do.

'It's too hot to go now. Maybe later this afternoon about four o'clock,' he replied.

'But that's too late. We need to go now,' John insisted.

'You won't get a driver to take you now,' he said as he drove off. We couldn't understand it. We were offering good money, it was not really that hot, and yet the taxi driver was right, no one would take us until later in the day. The best arrangement we could make was to be picked up at the hotel at 3 pm. In the meantime we set off on foot to explore the town.

The name Matadi means 'stone' in the local Kikongo language. It seemed a fitting name for this town clinging to a series of rocky outcrops with steep streets winding over stony hills. Walking down to the dock area past warehouses and dark shops, we could see the cranes, sheds and railway sidings of the port. Nothing moved. The cranes were still, the engines silent. Perhaps it was considered too hot to work. The only thing moving was the Zaïre River, rushing past on its relentless journey to the sea, now only 80 miles away. It was close to this spot that Stanley and his men came ashore in 1887 to begin their journey across the continent. Matadi is the main port of Zaïre, situated only a few hundred yards upstream from the border with Angola. It was a Portuguese sea captain, Diogo Caõ, who became the first European to venture up the Congo River in 1484, attempting to find an easy route into Central Africa. He met with disappointment shortly after passing Matadi when he found his way blocked by huge rapids, which were to prove an insurmountable obstacle to exploration for the next 300 years. Not until Stanley pioneered an overland route in 1877 was a way into the interior opened up.

Climbing back up the hill from the river into the centre of town, we began to understand why the heat was such an important factor in these parts. When the day began to cool a little, our hired taxi picked us up at the hotel and we set off to explore further afield. It was not long before we fell into the trap. On the north bank of the Zaïre River, beyond the long sweep of the new Field Marshal Mobutu Bridge, stood a large white monument of severe modernity in a parking area with an enticing viewpoint over the water. Surprised and pleased by this unexpected facility, we got out of the taxi and began enthusiastically photographing the town and port of Matadi on the far bank. The soldiers must have been lying in wait behind the monument. Now, brandishing automatic weapons and, ominously, a pair of handcuffs, they came running towards us.

'No photographs allowed give me your camera you are under arrest this is a serious offence', shouted the first soldier without pausing for breath, his expression one of mixed glee and triumph.

How long had he been waiting for such a heaven-sent opportunity, we wondered. With one camouflage-uniformed companion on each arm, John was marched back to the monument, unwilling prize in their private game.

'Passports!'

Silence fell as these were closely examined. Then, finding a clean page in an exercise book produced from his pocket, Number One soldier laboriously entered up our names and nationality.

'Which company do you work for in Zaïre?'

'We're tourists.'

There was evident disappointment at this response, which led to swift discussion in Lingala between the two men. Our command of Lingala is small, but as the conversation was laced with large numbers in French it was not difficult to surmise that they were talking about money.

'What are you doing here?' was their next question.

John's limited French had so far stood the test but now he handed over to me. As chief interpreter I always had to handle the difficult situations.

'Well,' I began, 'we're following the route of the British explorer Stanley and want to cross your beautiful country from west to east. We love your great river, magnificent mountains and above all the friendly, hospitable Zaïrean people.'

This little speech did not, alas, produce the desired effect. The soldiers merely looked blank.

'Show them the letter,' John said, playing our trump card.

At the Zaïre Embassy in London, the ambassador had been kind enough to give us a very authoritative-looking letter explaining what we were doing and requesting that assistance be offered to us along the way. Best of all, it was impressively headed and covered in official stamps. The soldiers fingered it gingerly for a while and then held a second debate.

'It may be possible to regularise the situation,' they reported finally.

This was to some extent good news as in Zaïre 'regularise' means that a pay-off will be accepted. So now it was just a question of how much—or how little—we could get away with. In these situations we have found that subtlety only leads to confusion and wasted time, so we adopted the direct approach.

'How much do you want?'

A figure had evidently already been arrived at as the response was immediate.

'3,000 zaïres.'

An expectant smile lit up the soldier's face. As this was the equivalent of about three months' pay, there was no chance of our handing over that sort of sum. John gave what he hoped was a convincingly light-hearted laugh and got down in earnest to the financial negotiations.

'I'll give you 250 zaïres.'

Their faces fell in disappointment. The bargaining went on until a compromise figure of 800 zaïres was reached. Then, just to make it appear that there had been some point to the whole affair, they insisted on confiscating the film from our camera. Now they were all smiles and friendly concern for the success of our journey in Zaïre. As we made off hurriedly in our taxi, Number Two soldier could be seen running happily down the road into town to get in beer supplies, which we had kindly sponsored, to ease the long hours of waiting before the next unsuspecting tourist walked into the trap.

The main objective of our trip that day was to reach the village of Vivi. When Stanley had returned to the Congo in 1879 to establish the Congo Free State on behalf of King Leopold of the Belgians, Vivi had for a time been its capital. It was rumoured that there was a small museum there and the remains of the *Lady Alice*, the sectional metal boat used by Stanley in his first descent of the Congo River. However, this was John's fifth visit to the area and despite various attempts he had never reached the elusive Vivi, nor for that matter ever met anyone else who had. After numerous enquiries along the road, we eventually found ourselves inspecting a narrow muddy trail that wound away into the hills. There was no prospect of getting the taxi along this track and much to the driver's relief an obliging local gave us the news that a bridge had collapsed further up. Closer enquiry also established that Vivi was about three and a half miles away. As it was already 5 o'clock and only an hour of daylight remained, the option of walking was also ruled out.

Retreating to the taxi, we contented ourselves with a drive along the main road and the occasional sortie to snatch a picture of the countryside, river and town on the opposite bank. Whilst we were engaged on one of these furtive photographic missions, a grey Peugeot car roared round a bend in the road and screeched to a halt in front of our taxi.

A man in his forties, wearing a long white Arab-style caftan and embroidered skull cap, leapt from the car, accompanied by a lad in jeans and T-shirt, and immediately demanded that John hand over the camera. I was still sitting in the taxi so John quickly passed the camera in to me. It had been a frustrating, not to say expensive, afternoon and we were in

no mood for a repeat of our earlier experience.

'Give me the camera,' the man repeated insistently.

'No. Who are you?'

'I'm a police officer. Give me your camera immediately.'

John looked with suspicion at his caftan and his companion's T-shirt.

'No. Show me your identity papers.'

I stuck my head out of the car window, scrutinised the card he produced, then announced, 'There's no mention of "police" on this. It's just an ordinary citizen's identity card.'

The man turned purple and began to stutter. No one had ever questioned his authority in this cavalier fashion before.

'Is this man a police officer?' John asked, turning to our taxi driver, who by this time was doing a good imitation of the invisible man.

'Yes,' he whispered.

Well, all right, we were ready to concede that the man probably was a policeman, but we were still not about to hand over our camera if we could possibly avoid it. We offered to accompany him back to town either in his car or in ours, but one thing was certain, we would not part with our equipment.

'Why won't you give me the camera?' he shouted finally in exasperation.

'Because you probably want to steal it,' I answered immediately with more frankness than diplomacy. This was the last straw. I thought our man was about to explode.

'All right. This could have been settled on the spot, but now you are in real trouble,' he thundered. 'Take them to my office. I'll be following behind,' he ordered the taxi driver.

With that we all set off back towards Matadi. At the toll barrier on the Mobutu Bridge the policeman called the official and ordered him not to let us across, then drove off fast in the direction from which we had just come.

We didn't have long to wait. Soon the Peugeot was back, this time with an additional passenger. Jumping from the car, Number One soldier from the monument ran over to our taxi, pushed the muzzle of his rifle through the window and repeated the words that had become so familiar to us that day, 'Give me your camera.' His was the most convincing argument we'd yet heard. I tend to become argumentative in these situations, but John decided that now was not the time to test his theory that Zaïrean soldiers are not allowed any ammunition for their guns. He handed the camera over meekly.

'Get out of the car and open the camera bag.'

We had been dreading this moment. The majority of our film stock—over 40 reels—was in the bag and such a horde would be sure to confirm our guilt as saboteurs and spies, if this was what they had decided we were. Sure enough, as soon as the bag was opened, a look of wide-eyed amazement came over the soldier's face. Gathering up the film to take over to the boss, he still had the presence of mind to slip two reels into his pocket. He was really having quite a good day.

The policeman sat stony-faced as the camera and films were loaded on to the back seat of his car. We were now convinced that this was the last we would see of them. John made a show of counting the reels, all the time protesting that he should accompany the policeman to the station. Then he remembered the letter. Our trump card hadn't won the game for us last time, but it was worth playing again since we had nothing to lose.

'Look here, we're on an officially sanctioned visit. We have permission to be in Zaïre and to take photographs.' I thrust the letter at him. He looked at it with disdain for a moment, then returned it to me without a word and scribbled a note of his own on a scrap of paper which he handed to our driver. 'Take them to my office,' he commanded. 'They will wait for me there.'

It was not far to the office. The taxi stopped a little way off; we paid the driver and with obvious relief he turned the car around and sped away, glad to see the last of such troublesome customers. The building he pointed out to us was just a normal suburban villa with no official sign outside. Only the fact that a uniformed guard sat in front of it and a number of sharply-dressed young men lounged around it singled out the place as one associated with security. We handed over our note. One of the smart young men looked at it then poked it under a locked door. 'The chief is not here at the moment. You'd better wait.'

'What time are you expecting him?'

'I can't say. He's gone to Mass.'

This didn't seem a very likely story, but as this place was our only contact with our photographic equipment, we decided we would have to wait to see the chief and get matters sorted out as soon as possible. A further complication was that we had to be in Kinshasa on Sunday morning if we were to have any chance of getting tickets for the river boat. That meant we had to leave Matadi before 10 o'clock on Saturday morning. It was Saturday tomorrow. Time was getting a little tight.

A wooden bench was brought outside and we settled down to wait. We have always found that waiting plays a major part in African travel. Dusk came and went, leaving us sitting in the gloom, our only companion the young soldier perched on his chair. On closer inspection we saw that the chair had no seat and kept expecting him to fall through, but he never did. We sat on, staring silently into the night. No sign of the policeman, the chief or our camera equipment. After two and a half hours it was clear that nothing was to be gained by waiting longer. We decided to return to the hotel. This was a slightly testing moment, as we did not know what the policeman's note had said and thus whether we were actually under arrest or not. Our dilemma was not immediately resolved when the guard insisted on returning to the hotel with us. We wondered whether we were to be submitted to the humiliation of sitting manacled to the soldier in the dining room. But no, his was a purely mercenary concern for our safety. The performance of this service cost us another 100 zaïres. We hoped the expenditure pattern established during our first four days in Zaïre was not going to be repeated throughout the country.

In our experience of Africa, the 'right time' simply doesn't exist; you are either too early or too late. Too late means arriving at the scheduled time to find that the boat, plane, train or man you arranged to meet has already left. Being too early requires your attendance as many hours before the scheduled time as possible to make sure there are no missed appointments or connections. The latter is the system adopted by Africans themselves. At any railway station, airport or bus depot, you can see groups of people who appear to be permanent residents, but who are simply making quite sure that they are on hand when the random decision is taken to depart. This may well involve days of waiting, but in this context time is an insignificant commodity. To be late can be a disaster, the destruction of one's best-laid plans at a single stroke, whereas to be early is just an inconvenience, and one which can often be turned to advantage. A shared wait can mean a shared conversation, an opportunity to meet people.

Following the early-bird principle, we arrived at the villa as the first tentative glow of dawn was pushing against the night sky. We had by this time learnt that we were not in the hands of the police or the army, but of a department known as the CENERIE which controls all travel by Zaïrean nationals at home and abroad as well as keeping a check on foreigners visiting or living in the country. It was widely regarded as a branch of the secret police. John and I had got our journey off to a splendid start by getting on the wrong side of these people, who certainly had the power to confiscate our photographic equipment, if they had not already done so, and to throw us out of the country if they felt so inclined. I polished up a few conciliatory phrases in French as we planned a low-key approach, very different from yesterday's confrontation.

It was just before 7 am when we arrived. None of the staff was yet on duty, but the soldier on guard let us into the ground-floor office to wait. It was a small bare room containing only a table, an old typewriter, a chair and the bench on which we had spent so many hours the night before. The dark grease stain along the wall above the bench testified to the number of people who had waited in this office over the years, just as we were doing now. At around 7.30 am the first of the staff began arriving for work. By 8 o'clock our bench had filled up with six more supplicants, all grasping sheaves of papers and looking apprehensive, like a group of job applicants waiting to be interviewed. Attempts at conversation soon petered out as everyone was reluctant to say anything that might conceivably compromise their chances in front of the man who had now stationed himself at the desk and was doing battle with the ancient typewriter.

One of the snappy dressers we had seen last night arrived for work. Saturday was evidently a casual day. His smart suit was now replaced by vivid green trousers and a T-shirt with 'Im a big boy' emblazoned somewhat ungrammatically across the chest.

'Hello. Still here?' he said with a grin.

'Afraid so,' I replied glumly. It didn't seem a good idea to appear too cocky about the situation.

'Are you the ones with all that camera equipment?'

'Yes, have you seen it?' I enquired with some interest.

'It's up in the chief's office. It must be worth a lot of money.'

'Oh no, it's not an expensive camera,' I replied hastily, not wishing to encourage the idea that it was a major prize. At least our equipment was here and that must, we assumed, be good news.

There were various comings and goings, but no one took much notice of us. Time was marching on. It was gone 9 o'clock and we still hoped to get back to Kinshasa that night. Saturday's train had already left and the only other route out of Matadi was the bus scheduled to leave at 10 o'clock. It was 9.20 am when another man hurried into the room and beckoned to us.

'The chief will see you now. Come this way.'

Taking a deep breath, we followed the man up a flight of stairs and along a yellow-painted passage to a blank white door at the end. Our guide knocked deferentially and waited. 'Enter,' came the command from inside. The door opened on to a cool green room. The curtains were drawn against the sharp sunlight and an air-conditioning unit laboured noisily under the window. A small table to the left was stacked high with our film and camera equipment and straight ahead, seated behind an imposing executive desk, was the chief in the process of studying our passports. Our hearts sank. The chief was none other than the man who had picked us up yesterday. This was not a good start. We stood in silence before the desk, on our best behaviour, not speaking until spoken to.

'Check the camera equipment,' said the chief abruptly.

'It all seems fine,' John replied, quickly looking it over.

'Count the films.'

'Oh, I'm sure that won't be necessary.'

'Count them.'

John counted them. 'Forty. All in order.'

'None missing?'

'None.'

'So am I a thief?'

I was ready to go into action at this point with Mission Conciliation.

'Certainly not, sir. We can only offer our apologies for the stupid misunderstanding of yesterday. It was our fault entirely....'

My sentence trailed away as his raised hand cut me off. He continued to study our passports, reading each page with close attention. We tried to think back over recent travels to see if there was any country to which Zaïre could possibly take exception. Cold beads of sweat ran down the inside of our arms as we contemplated immediate deportation or worse.

'There are a number of serious matters to be considered here,' said the chief, paying out the line as the fish squirmed at the end of it. 'Photographing strategic installations, in this case the port and the bridge, no proper permit for the camera, and last, but not least, insulting an officer.'

There didn't seem much to say at this point, so we contented ourselves with looking contrite. But suddenly the chief seemed bored with the whole affair. He had had his revenge for yesterday. We were very small fish and there was nothing more to be gained from us. The line slipped free.

'I will take no further action in this case. You notified the authorities in Kinshasa, but unfortunately the information was not passed on to my office here in Matadi. Give me the film from the camera then you can go.'

No arguments today. We would lose our shots, but John quickly removed the film and handed it over. We stuffed the camera and packets of film into a plastic bag we had optimistically brought along for the purpose and, with expressions of gratitude and profuse apology, turned and made our escape.

There were a few surprises awaiting us at the Matadi bus-stop, and all of them pleasant. Firstly, in spite of arriving five minutes after the scheduled departure time of the Kinshasa bus, we were for once early. The bus pulled in at 10.30 am. Secondly, the bus itself was a spanking new Mercedes that would not have looked out of place on a German autobahn; and thirdly, it was not even full. There was every prospect of a quiet, comfortable and uneventful trip to the capital. After the experiences of the last few days, that was all we asked. Matadi had been a waste of time from almost every point of view. We had failed to reach any of the places we had hoped to see, had spent a large part of our time waiting in security offices, had lost virtually all the photographs we had taken and had come close to aborting the whole trip before it had even begun. We were glad to be leaving Matadi.

The bus climbed up into the bare hills of the Crystal Mountains and we settled back to enjoy the journey. As the town slipped away behind us, we began to relax and appreciate the pleasure of a new departure. After all, up to now we had done no more than arrive at our starting point. The bus marked the beginning of our crossing of Africa. The months of planning and the struggle to get to the starting gate were over. The whole of the conti-nent lay before us. That was an encouraging idea.

*****

We were at this point following Stanley's route not only in a general, but in a specific sense. The forerunner of the road we were travelling on had been forced through these unrelenting hills by Stanley himself, or rather under his drive and direction. Within two years of his struggling out of the African bush after his 999-day crossing of the continent in 1877, Stanley returned to found the Congo Free State on behalf of King Leopold. His first task was to build a route from Matadi to Stanley Pool to by-pass the 220 miles of rapids that separate the two. The construction of this track was the key to the opening up of the interior of Africa. It not only

The SS Madura *unloads at Banana Point at the mouth of the Congo River.*

33

enabled caravans of porters to make the journey to the Pool in a reasonable time, but, more importantly, steam boats to be brought up in pieces, assembled at the Pool and used to explore and trade along the upper reaches of the Congo River and its thousands of miles of tributaries.

When Stanley came ashore at Matadi in March 1887 to start his last African adventure, the track he had built was in place, but it was to prove no easy task to move a caravan of nearly 1000 people and tons of equipment along it to Stanley Pool. This was a testing time for Stanley and his European officers, for whom the great expedition had so far consisted of a pleasant cruise, first to Zanzibar then to South Africa and on up the west coast to the mouth of the Congo. The reality of overland travel seems to have come as something of a shock to the officers. Their experiences on this march mark the start of a breakdown in the relationship between themselves and their leader, particularly serious in the case of the expedition's second-in-command, Major Edmund Barttelot. Stanley's methods of working had nothing to do with the niceties of behaviour taught at the good schools which his gentlemen officers had attended. From Jameson's diary we have a few illustrations of what it was like on the road. Three weeks into the march and we have an example of Stanley dealing with a dispute in camp:

. . . some of the Sudanese and Zanzibaris began fighting about a cooking pot, and awoke Mr Stanley, who was sleeping. He seized a stick, ran in, and whacked away right and left, giving one fellow a regular facer with his fist . . . .

Jameson evidently did not think much of the sort of work he was expected to do:

The march from Matadi was one of the most disgusting pieces of work I have ever had to do . . . a lot of slave drivers of the old school would have done it much better, for that—slave-driving—is what it often resolved itself into.

Stanley and the expedition on the march from Matadi to Leopoldville.

To make matters worse, poor Jameson had actually paid for the privilege of being a slave driver. Nor did he think highly of Stanley's handiwork as a road builder, commenting that it was '. . . one of the worst roads I have ever seen, up and down masses of cinder-like rock and broken quartz.'

When it comes to his opinion of Stanley, he seems to be in a state of ambivalence. On one day he writes in a huff about the way Stanley treats his officers: 'It is impossible for any one calling himself

34

a gentleman, and an officer, to stand this sort of thing. The fact is, this is the first time Stanley has ever had gentlemen to deal with on an expedition of this sort.' But two days later he seems to have changed his mind: 'Mr Stanley, when he throws off his reserve, is one of the most agreeable of men and full of information.'

What, perhaps, Jameson and the other officers did not realise was that, in Stanley's view, it needed at least a year for a European new to handling natives to be of any use to him. This would have been a frustrating time for Stanley, with so many problems on his mind, and on top of everything a group of officers who could not even speak to their men and who would need a long period of licking into shape.

It must have seemed like a godsend to Stanley when, on the fourth day out, over the hill towards him marched Herbert Ward, a man whom he knew well, and who had already proved his worth whilst working for him during his governorship of the Congo Free State. The 24-year-old Ward had served two and a half years in the Congo and was on his way home when he heard of Stanley's expedition and decided to join it. From his previous experience he knew that actions, not words, would impress Stanley. Porters would be needed so he hired 400 and set off. He was told that if he could move the thousand loads still at Matadi up to Leopoldville (present-day Kinshasa) in a month, Stanley would 'take him along'. Happily Ward set off. A new officer had been enrolled on the expedition.

John Rose Troup, the transport officer who had shipped out to the Congo in advance of the expedition, was stationed at Manyanga, the halfway point on the march. His task was to forward to Leopoldville the loads that were not carried by the main group. He busied himself keeping a flow of fresh porters coming in to take over the loads as they arrived from Matadi. Eventually Ward and Troup joined forces and arrived in Leopoldville

on the last day of April, precisely on schedule.

*****

The afternoon was hot. Whilst the bus was on the move it was pleasant, with a good breeze keeping the temperature at a comfortable level, but as soon as we stopped the interior was like an oven. We stopped often, but mercifully usually only for a couple of minutes, a few passengers getting off, a few more getting on, at the windows children offering bananas, hard-boiled eggs and drinks for sale. At one or two stops, local produce—manioc, potatoes, pineapples, chickens and the like—was on offer. A woman sitting across the aisle from us was designed in the classic African mould, weighing about 20 stone, dressed in swathes of brightly coloured cloth covered in pictures of Mobutu, 'founder of the nation', her hair wound with black thread and fashioned into a dozen spiky antennae. A plump hand gripped a large piece of green cloth with which she constantly staunched the flow of sweat from her huge face. Her voice, as big as her body, boomed around the bus and her laugh, an awesome sound, proved seriously damaging to the health when directed at you at point-blank range.

The world slipped past the window: hilly country with open grassland, patches of scrub, and in the hollows and along the rivers fresh green slashes of vegetation that brightened the drab, sun-bleached savannah.

Late in the afternoon we entered the outskirts of Kinshasa, passing busy markets and long lines of open-fronted shops. Then, breasting a hill in the exclusive residential district of Binza, the city and the hazy river lay before us. On the left, through high railings, okapi, antelopes and other examples of Zaïre's wildlife could be seen grazing in the secure parkland that forms the grounds of the presidential palace on Mount N'Galiema. For half an hour the bus toured the suburbs, dropping off passengers at markets and intersections until at last we drew into the bus station just off the main street, Boulevard du 30 Juin. It had taken just six and a half hours to reach Kinshasa from Matadi. A hundred years before it had not been so easy for Stanley who had taken 29 days to cover the same distance, and that was considered good going for the time. On arrival, Stanley's preoccupation, like ours, was with the availability of river transport, a problem he managed to resolve in nine days of hectic activity. Tomorrow we would see if we could improve on his performance.

Congo River

King Leopold's brave promise of the use of his Congo River flotilla materialised as one boat in working order, the *Stanley*, and a few shells without power that could be used as barges. Since it would be impossible to move the expedition upstream with this meagre fleet, it was essential to obtain use of the boats belonging to the American and English Baptist missions at Leopoldville. As the situation was further complicated by a severe shortage of food in the district, Major Barttelot was immediately dispatched up river in the *Stanley* with as many men as possible to await the expedition in an area where food was more plentiful.

In the meantime, Stanley set about the missionaries. Whilst still in England he had applied for, and been refused, permission to use the English mission boat. Luckily, Mr Bentley, the missionary, was not aware of this and reluctantly handed over the *Peace*.

The Americans were a more difficult case. They refused to have any dealings with Stanley, whom they considered the devil's agent, and had no wish to be associated with his methods in the eyes of the natives. The presence of Tippu Tip in the party could not have helped Stanley's cause. In the end Lieutenant Liebriechts, the commander of Leopoldville Station, requisitioned the *Henry Reed* for the State and handed it over to Stanley. It was very much in his interests to see the expedition out of his sphere of responsibility before famine gripped his whole area.

Having begged, borrowed or purloined all the available shipping, the expedition and its equipment still could not be fully accommodated. Two trips would be necessary. The plan was to leave a group of men at Bolobo, higher up the river, where food was no problem, while some 500 loads would stay at Leopoldville under the care of Troup, the transport officer. After taking the major part of the expedition to the Aruwimi River, one of the boats would return, pick up these loads and the men from Bolobo and then catch up with the main party.

Stanley's first thought was to leave Major Barttelot at Bolobo, presumably to keep him out of the way. The relationship between the two men was not good. The Major had been appointed second-in-command on the basis of his military rank. He had commanded in the field and did not feel any need to be 'licked into shape'. Stanley, on the other hand, was looking for a deputy who followed orders, not a man such as Barttelot who he feared would act on his own initiative. The lack of shipping had necessitated the re-thinking of tactics. A base camp would have to be established on the Aruwimi and men and equipment left there to await the arrivals from Bolobo and Leopoldville. In the meantime, an advance column would press on to the relief of Emin Pasha.

The appearance of Ward on the scene was a further complication. It was he who was chosen to travel in the same boat as Stanley. To the others it seemed that this interloper was very likely to be preferred over themselves. At one stage Barttelot was certain that Ward would replace him as second-in-command. Whatever Stanley's feelings on the matter, he had his own sense of fair play and allowed himself to be persuaded not to leave Barttelot at Bolobo. In the end it was Ward and Bonny who were abandoned in the wilderness, whilst Barttelot was awarded the second least desirable task, the command of the Rear Column at the Aruwimi River base camp.

On 1 May 1887 the flotilla set sail. There were three boats under power, the *Stanley*, the *Henry Reed* and the *Peace*, towing an assortment of five barges and hulls. Stanley's boat, the *Peace*, was the last to leave but, as he wrote, '. . . the good wishes of the people on shore had scarcely died away, and we were breasting the rapid current, when her rudder snapped in two.' He had to endure the embarrassment of an immediate return to port for repairs and, no doubt, the smug smiles of one or two men of God. The next day he was under way again, and the expedition was on the move northwards.

*****

It is never an easy matter trying to set out up country from Kinshasa. Enquiries at the port had revealed that two boats regularly plied the 1000 miles of river between Kisangani (Stanley Falls) and the capital. The *Colonel Tshatshi* was in dock awaiting repairs, the *Colonel Kokolo* out of contact, somewhere in the vast green tracts of equatorial rain forest. We had put our names on the reserve list for a first-class cabin before leaving for Matadi and now awaited the *Kokolo*'s return.

Kinshasa is a fine town to spend time in if you have plenty of money and your own transport. We had neither and we hated it. We spent quite a lot of time walking around the hot, dusty streets of the centre. We should have known better. On a quiet Sunday afternoon in a street not far from the Memling Hotel, we walked towards a group of boys playing football. As we approached, the numbers suddenly swelled, a youth pulled out a knife, crying 'Your money!', and the rest of the gang jumped on John. His leather bag was torn from his grasp, and his arm gashed in the struggle. He sensibly decided to cut his losses and put up no resistance, but I waded into the fray, grabbing the bag and tugging for all I was worth. It was torn away, leaving me holding only the leather strap and having suffered several scratches and bruises. As the gang ran off I realised I hadn't been very sensible and might easily have fared a lot worse. As they ran, our attackers scattered papers, credit cards and, luckily for us, our traveller's cheques. They even threw down the bag. All they were interested in were the zaïre notes, and they did well, for we had 16,000 zaïres in cash, the equivalent of £300, in readiness for buying our boat tickets.

On the way back to the hotel we discovered that John's Rolex watch had been stolen, too. I think he felt that more than the loss of the money as he had had the watch since our first expedition in Zaïre 12 years earlier.

The hotel receptionist told us that if he'd known what we were doing he would have advised us—of course—that it was not safe to walk the streets alone, especially on a Sunday.
'Should we report the robbery to the police?' John asked.
'No, there's no point. They are not like the police in your country. Here they are not serious,' he said with a dismissive laugh.

Our luck turned after this episode, for which we were thankful. Things had not been going well for us up to now. The *Colonel Kokolo* arrived in port. In total we had waited only a week. People have been known to wait three or four weeks and sometimes even longer. By that time, too, a 'luxury-class' cabin had become available, equipped, we were told, with air-conditioning and private bathroom. It sounded too good to be true. We followed the chief accommodation officer as he forced a way through the booking hall to the row of ticket clerks struggling to cope with the tide of humanity that threatened at any moment to engulf them. Feeling rather conspicuous, we passed through a guarded door and entered one of the glass-fronted cubicles from the rear. The clerk interrupted his frantic activity to write out two tickets, throwing our money into a vast tin trunk at his feet. Then it was back to selling third-class tickets, taking money from hands pushed through a round aperture and tossing tickets over the top of the glass partition, where they were expertly caught by the successful applicants.

Next day the taxi made its way slowly through the crowds at the port gates and deposited us and our rucksacks on the dock. We gingerly mounted the swaying gangway and found, rather to our surprise, that our names were actually on the passenger list and a cabin had been allocated to us. We put down our packs and surveyed our new home. The cabin seemed spacious, owing to the fact that there were only two chairs and a single bed in it. The second bed was standing in several pieces in a corner. There was no sign of air-conditioning, but there was indeed a bathroom. The toilet wouldn't flush, there was no light, but the shower worked and magically brought forth hot water.
'Yes, yes, you'll have a bed very soon.'
The purser looked harassed as we enquired for the third time about our sleeping arrangements. In fact the nearest we ever got to a complete bed was mid-way through the voyage when a double wooden bedhead appeared mysteriously outside our cabin door, stayed there a few days, then just as mysteriously disappeared again. However, on this first day we were given a foam mattress and

two sheets and John slept quite happily on the floor for the rest of the journey. The smiling purser presented us with a light bulb for the bathroom and a bucket to flush the toilet, and all was well. The only remaining problem, which did not become obvious until the engines started up and we got under way, was that one wall of our cabin adjoined the main funnel. For a cruise around the northern ports of Europe in mid-winter, the temperature in the cabin would have been ideal, but for an equatorial river boat it proved a little steamy.

Having explored our quarters, we went out on deck to watch the scene of chaos below us on the dock. Every square inch was filled with passengers, porters, children, trunks, sacks, mattresses, suites of furniture wrapped in sacking and unidentifiable bundles of all shapes and sizes. Like a column of ants on the march, heavily-laden men and women staggered down the narrow gangplank, while those returning empty-handed squeezed past on their way up for more. Even when the *Kokolo*'s stern began to pull away from the dock, the last of the passengers were to be seen running frantically to the prow, where helping hands hauled them aboard. Once out in the river, the *Kokolo* performed a kind of square dance as she manoeuvred her partners from side to side. A Zaïre river boat is not a single vessel, but a motley assortment of floating parts. The main boat, a high white five-deck vessel, contains the first- and luxury-class cabins, the bridge and engine room, and propels a number of barges which house around 1500 second- and third-class passengers together with the freight. By the time the *Kokolo* had completed her manoeuvres, we had one barge lashed in front and two on either side, and were at last ready to set off.

Above Kinshasa the river opens out into the 20-mile-wide, island-strewn Pool Malebo, formerly Stanley Pool, where the *Kokolo* with her numerous encumbrances made slow progress against the strong current. At the head of the pool we passed between high white cliffs where the river is compressed by the rock walls of the Crystal Mountains in a channel only half a mile wide. Dug-out canoes, with their makeshift sails raised, took advantage of the strong winds blowing upstream to keep abreast of the chugging river boat.

Two days and 200 miles further on, we reached the small town of Bolobo, where Ward and Bonny had temporarily been

For the village of Bolobo, the river boats are the main contact with the outside world. Trading is fast and furious on the Kokolo's *arrival.*

41

abandoned 100 years before. The scene changed dramatically as the mountains fell away and the river eased itself to a width of between eight and twelve miles. Islands large and small dotted its surface, forest trees covered its banks and marched away into the distance. From our vantage point high up on the *Kokolo*, we looked out over waters that shimmered under the relentless sun, over a vibrant green backdrop in which every tree looked as if lovingly hand-painted, to a vast horizon where river melted into blue-grey sky. It was hard to comprehend the menace which oppressed the river boat captain in Joseph Conrad's *Heart of Darkness*, based on the writer's own brief experience on the Congo in 1890:

The long stretches of waterway ran on, deserted, into the gloom of overshadowed distances . . . this stillness of life did not in the least resemble peace. It was the stillness of an implacable force brooding over an inscrutable intention. It looked at you with vengeful aspect.

*****

One of Stanley's officers, Jephson, took a similarly jaundiced view of the river: 'It is peculiar what a feeling of hatred the river inspires one with. One hates it as if it were a living thing . . . .'

Of course his journey was nothing like as comfortable as ours, and there was the added burden of gathering fuel for the wood-burning steamers. Stanley details the requirments for a day's sailing for one boat:

. . . it would require 50 men to search for and carry wood for quite two hours; it would re-

Cutting wood to keep the steamers supplied was a nightly chore.

quire a dozen axemen to cut it up into 30-inch lengths for the grate . . . It must be stored on board the steamers that no delay might take place in the morning.

This was a task that often continued late into the night. Even Jameson, the man whom everyone complimented on his continual good humour, joined in the general depression: 'I have never been on a trip where there is so little enjoyment of any kind; it is all so serious, and a kind of gloom hangs over all.'

*****

The *Kokolo* formed a moving island of noise and colour which kept at bay any suggestion of gloom. On the tightly-packed second- and third-class barges many of the passengers were resident traders who carried on their daily routine much as they would at home, washing clothes, soaping children and cooking, their stalls neatly laid out along the narrow gang-ways that laced the barges. Our first im-pression was one of general confusion, but on closer inspection all was seen to be carefully ordered. One area specialised in second-hand clothing, each garment assigned its particular pile—shorts, trousers, dresses, blouses, skirts, coats and bras—the choicest items displayed on lines slung overhead. Another area concentrated on medicines and cos-metics—soaps, lotions, razor blades, mir-rors, combs and brightly coloured pills in long plastic strips dispensed in any quantity to suit the customer's purse. Next door in the restaurant and take-away section, fish were prepared, rice washed and fat white grubs roasted over charcoal burners. Beyond that was the bar and dance hall where quantities of warm Primus, the local beer, were sunk to the accompaniment of the compelling rhythms of drum and electric guitar, the pop music of Zaïre that has spread all over Africa.

Life in first class was very different. The passengers seemed to consist in large part of officials of ONATRA, the national transport company which operates the river boats. In many cases they and their families were making the three-week round trip as a holiday. As they generally took their meals in their cabins, the large air-conditioned dining room was often thinly populated. Regular attenders were the half-dozen European passengers who congregated at one of the long tables for meals of meat, potatoes or rice, and vegetables, all professionally served by waiters in white jackets. The food was very much better than we had antici-pated, but strangely, on a river teeming with fish, the latter never appeared on the menu. It seemed that fish was acceptable for the lower orders, but was definitely out as far as first-class passengers were concerned. To sample the local fish, we had to resort to buying one and paying the cook to prepare it for us. Our travel-ling companions were Alain, a Belgian, and Peter, a Swiss, two young men work-ing in Dubai who had taken six months off to make a sponsored trip through Africa; and Thomas and Karin, a young German couple doing Africa on the cheap, who had decided to splash out on a first-class cabin for the ten-day river trip. Thrown together by circumstance, we got on well and enjoyed each other's company enormously.

One of our Zaïrean neighbours had a portable television, along with a huge number of trunks which filled his single cabin and overflowed on to the deck out-side. A great crowd gathered round the television on the night that Morocco beat Portugal in the World Cup. '*Maroc! Maroc!*' The cries echoed across the dark river. The signal weakened as we got further from Kinshasa until eventually the World Cup was left behind in a dif-ferent world.

Onboard entertainment was excellent and non-stop. There were the market stalls of the second- and third-class barges to be visited, titbits, such as crispy fried caterpillar, from the take-away stalls to be tried, and constant activity on the river itself. At all times of the day and night, local fishermen paddled out to the

Evening finds the steamer lying off Lukalela.

After hitting a sand bank, a third-class barge breaks free from the Colonel Kokolo *and leaves the traders aboard temporarily stranded.*

Kokolo with their catches of huge, flat-headed, be-whiskered Captain fish, a type of catfish often weighing in at over 100 lb. The name was appropriate since the ship's captain was himself, in a private capacity, the chief buyer of fish and had his agent permanently stationed by the deck rail to spot incoming giants and order their owners to take them to the bridge for inspection. This was unfortunate for the fishermen concerned as they had to drag 100 lb of fish up five steep staircases to the wheelhouse and were then obliged to accept whatever price the captain cared to offer. It became apparent that this was the captain's chief interest in the voyage. He had a cold room bigger than a cabin at his disposal and soon had it filled to overflowing with fish which he intended to sell at 300 to 400 per cent profit in the market at Kisangani.

It would be unfair to suggest that the captain's absorption in commerce was one of the reasons we hit so many sandbanks, for the river channels are notoriously changeable and shifting sandbars a constant navigational hazard. Some sandbanks we nosed into gently and were able to back off, but others were hit at speed, the impact causing the barges to break

free from the main boat. As the river has a strong current flowing at about eight knots, a barge without power was soon floating majestically back downstream and the *Kokolo* spent many hours scurrying to and fro in pursuit of her wayward charges.

For many of the villages and small towns we passed, the steamer provided the only link with the outside world. At our approach swarms of dug-out canoes converged on the boat to trade their produce of fish, fruit, vegetables and meat (antelope, monkey, goat, pig and crocodile) for the goods on sale on board. The paddlers had to use all their skill and judgement in attempting to board. They would wait upstream as the *Kokolo* approached, then at a shouted signal would start paddling furiously on an interception course, their paddles slicing through the water in unison like a well-oiled machine. If successful, they would strike the boat alongside the leading barge and would be swept down the side, caught in the wash. The man in the bow of the canoe had then to grab the deck rail to try to slow their progress before leaping athletically aboard with the painter in his hand. Dug-outs are heavy and

Many isolated fishing camps lie along the banks of the Zaïre River. People come from their forest villages in the interior to fish and trade for a few months before returning home.

A lone dug-out canoe and its crew wait poised to make a run to board the river boat, a manoeuvre that requires great skill and judgement as the current is swift and the steamer ploughs on regardless.

unstable and often capsized. There were also occasional complete misses when a team of paddlers, because of bad timing or an extra strong current, failed to board the boat altogether and were swept past, laughing and waving, to await the arrival of the next boat in a few weeks' time.

The warm cocoon of ship-board life closed pleasantly around us, interrupted only by stops at Mbandaka, Lisala and Bumba, the three main towns on the river route, where we were forced temporarily back into contact with the real world. This proved to be a world of pot-holed streets and decaying buildings populated by surly officials grasping at the opportunity to harass passing Europeans. Our expeditions ashore were short and usually fraught with problems and we were always glad to get back safely to the protected world of the *Colonel Kokolo*.

*****

On 30 May 1887 the expedition reached Bangala, 500 miles from Leopoldville at a point where the river makes a sharp turn to the east. Since the loss of Stanley Falls this was the last Congo Free State station on the river. The officers were greeted by Lieutenant van Kerckhoven, the flamboyant station commander with a taste for champagne and shoulder-length hair. Although the station was well established with its own food supplies, the arrival of the expedition must have been as welcome as a plague of locusts. There had already been trouble down river with the men looting native villages for food. This event had prompted a major row between Stanley and two of his officers, Jephson and Stairs, whom he had threatened to dismiss. The expedition did not linger long at Bangala. It split again with Major Barttelot being dispatched to deliver Tippu Tip to Stanley Falls, whilst the rest of the party made its way to the Aruwimi River.

Tippu was now entering his own territory, but his people knew nothing of his arrangement with King Leopold nor of his return, and initially fired on the steamer thinking it was the Free State forces coming to re-take Stanley Falls. Once this misunderstanding was cleared up, the talking drums spread the word and the rest of the voyage became a royal progress. The ruler had returned.

Before leaving the Falls to rejoin the main party, Barttelot tried to persuade Tippu to confirm the arrangements made with Stanley for the additional 600 porters whom he would need when the remaining loads came up river. Now Tippu claimed that the contract was broken because there was no ammunition to supply to his men as agreed. It was still at Bolobo. Barttelot's understanding was that a verbal agreement had been made between Stanley and Tippu that the latter would supply his own ammunition for which he would be paid later. The truth seems to be that on arriving at Stanley Falls, Tippu discovered that gunpowder was in short supply and very expensive and he was not prepared to pay the price. Barttelot sailed away thinking that he had an agreement for the provision of some 200 men who would arrive within the next two weeks. In reality this was just the beginning of the smoke-screen of confusion which the wily Arab was to spread and in which poor Barttelot would be lost for months to come.

The main expedition had arrived at the mouth of the Aruwimi River without incident, and on 12 June was lying off the large village of Basoko on the north bank. Here a little experiment in 'civilising' was put to the test. Stanley's native servant Baruti had been captured from this village seven years before and eventually taken to England, where he lived with Stanley for some years. Now he was given the opportunity to re-establish contact with his family and, if he chose, return to his home village. Baruti called his brother to the boat. At first the man was suspicious and did not recognise Baruti.

'If you are my brother, tell me some incident, that I may know you.'

'Thou hast a scar on thy arm—there, on

the right. Dost thou not remember the crocodile?'

Of course, his brother did remember and there was a touching scene of reunion. But it seemed that civilisation had more pull and Baruti loyally decided to stay with his master. It is notable that the tribe's deep hostility was not overcome, even with such a powerful calling card. They would neither trade nor allow the expedition to land. Baruti, it appeared, had learnt from his experiences in Europe as a few days later he disappeared, taking with him Stanley's rifle, two revolvers, ammunition, a watch and a pedometer. He evidently intended to be well-equipped in his new life.

*****

The *Kokolo* was running late; we did not reach our destination, Basoko, until the eleventh day out from Kinshasa. In fact, we nearly didn't reach it at all. The river was too shallow, the captain told us, for the boat to approach Basoko, 100 miles downstream from Kisangani. Instead he would have to stop at Lokutu, a little way upstream on the opposite bank where the water was deeper. So 1.30 am on 22 June found us standing by the deck rail with our rucksacks, peering down into the illuminated night and the pandemonium below. 'Basoko! Basoko!' The cries of the ferrymen drew our attention to a waiting rank of taxi *pirogues*. We selected one that had an outboard motor, bade farewell to our shipboard companions, fought our way over the rail and through the mêlée of bodies scrambling on and off the boat and finally heaved ourselves into our chosen dug-out. The men paddled the canoe at first, causing us to wonder if the engine was just for show. It was very peaceful on the dark river as we drew away from the noise and lights of the *Kokolo*, the only sounds the splashing of the paddles and the occasional spoken word. In deeper stretches of water, the motor was started up and an hour later we pulled quietly into Basoko, a million miles, or so it seemed, from our previous river-boat existence.

We were lucky in Basoko to meet up with Monteiro, the Portuguese manager of a Zaïrean trading company, who insisted that we stay with him until we could find onward transport. Having spent our first few hours in what passed for the local hotel, we were delighted to accept his invitation. His house had electric light and a 'condi' that came on in the evening (the term puzzled us at first until we realised it was the local abbreviation of air-conditioning), a hand-turned wheel in the yard which brought water up from the river, a large television and video unit, and a houseboy, Senga, whose name seemed to be synonymous with 'fetch'. 'Senga, beer!' 'Senga, water!' The cries issued from the open window and Senga would pad silently from his cook house down the yard to fetch whatever was required.

We came to regret the presence of the video. Duarte, a Portuguese friend of Monteiro's, arrived from Kisangani with the latest batch of video films. We had seen Clint Eastwood and his orang utan in *Every Which Way but Loose* in England and had enjoyed the film, but its attractions began to pale when we sat through it for the third time in Basoko. Monteiro

and Duarte fell off their chairs in mirth while the row of employees who gathered at the windows to watch the silent version and Senga and his friends, privileged to sit at the back of the room, laughed in a more subdued manner. Worse than *Every Which Way* were more films of the World Cup matches. This time cries of anguish went up when Morocco beat Portugal, except from the back of the room where muffled sniggers could be detected.

We explored the crumbling remains of Basoko's Congo Free State days: an old brick road, a crenellated wall, a decaying gateway, all part of the fort built by Lieutenant van Kerckhoven in the early 1890s against attacks by Arab slave traders. Beyond the fort lay the old cemetery, very overgrown, with only a few stones still standing. The names on most were indecipherable, but we were pleased to find one that was still very clear: George Grenfell born 1849, died 1 July 1906. Grenfell was a tireless missionary and explorer, whose former house at Bolobo we had stayed in briefly on an expedition on the Zaïre River 12 years earlier.

Monteiro's hospitality did not stop at offering accommodation. It was through his good offices that we finally began our

49

journey up the Aruwimi. We had met the two Italian and Polish priests at the Catholic Mission and learnt that the Pole, Father Mietek, was shortly to set out on a journey up river to visit remote villages in his parish. He had kindly offered us transport as far as the village of Mongandjo, but the day before we were due to set off, we heard from Mietek that the mission's outboard motor was kaput. Enquiries in the village revealed that the only *pirogue* with outboard available for hire at that time would cost us 8000 zaïres.

'Too much for me,' said Mietek gloomily.

'Too much for us,' we agreed.

So Mietek made plans to use the Mission Landrover and travel the long overland route. Again we were offered a lift. Again it was not to be. That same day word reached Basoko that the ferry on which we would have to cross the Aruwimi had broken down and was stuck on the far bank. Refusing to admit defeat, Mietek prepared to take the much longer north bank route, only to learn that a bridge was down and the road impassable. The devil certainly seemed to be putting obstacles in the way of the Lord's work.

Monteiro saved the day. He came in at lunch time, beaming.

'I've found you a *pirogue*. You leave at two this afternoon. I've sent a boy to the mission to tell Father Mietek. So let's have a beer and then lunch. Senga! Beer!' This was excellent news, but it would be as well to get the practicalities sorted out.

'How much is the boatman charging?' John asked.

'Oh, don't worry about that. I've fixed it with the man—he often works for me.' However hard we pressed, Monteiro wouldn't budge. He refused to let us or Mietek pay a penny. All we could do to try to repay the generous hospitality we had received was to invite him to be our guest in England when he made his next visit to Europe.

The *pirogue* was fully laden when we

set off. There were three boatmen (were they expecting to have to paddle?), the two of us and our rucksacks, Father Mietek and the moped he used to get from village to village, and Victor Mose and his bicycle. Victor, a Catholic pastor and family man from the village of Mongandjo, was returning home after a three-day parish training session at the Basoko Mission. He had kindly offered to help us on the next leg of our journey.

As we sliced through the shimmering water, the vivid mass of palms, trees and bushes on the river banks looked almost as if it had been landscaped. Kingfishers swooped and thick islands of mauve-flowered water hyacinth floated silently by. At one point we got stuck on a sand-bank and the men, rolling up their trousers, jumped in to push us free. Because of the danger of sandbars, the boatmen decided against travelling at night and as darkness fell we pulled in to the village of Ilongo-Koki where Mietek and Victor were well known to the members of the large Catholic community.

'*Mbote nayo.*'

'*Mbote nabino.*'

Lingala greetings rang out from all sides and we were welcomed into the house of Alphonse, the *chef de localité*.

We were off early next morning, the mist still lying low over the river and forest. A couple of hours later Victor instructed the boatmen to pull in at a small village. He took our historical researches seriously and had a surprise for us. This was the village of Likombe where, he told us, Stanley had fought a battle against the natives and been forced to withdraw. We met the grandson of Chief Bolita, the man responsible for Stanley's defeat, and were shown the actual shield his grandfather had used and the leopard-tooth necklace he had worn. Bolita, it seems, was a good business man. After first refusing to let Stanley pass, he later agreed terms with him that were advantageous to himself and his village. We were not altogether convinced of the historical accuracy of this episode as there appeared

51

The villagers of Likombe on the Aruwimi River give us a typically enthusiastic send-off.

to be no mention of it in the various records of the Emin Pasha Relief Expedition, but we were delighted that at last we had found some hearsay historical association with Stanley. In Kinshasa his statue had long since been pulled down, everywhere his name had been obliterated, and no one we had met so far could tell any stories of the man or his times that had been passed down to them.

Another of Victor's contributions to our researches was his account of the origins of the name 'Aruwimi': two natives in a *pirogue* at the mouth of the river were approached by Stanley who, in Swahili, asked its name. Neither man spoke Swahili and had never seen, let alone spoken to, a white man before. '*Aruwimi*? (Does he know me?)' said one to the other in the local language. Stanley, misunderstanding, wrote down 'Aruwimi' as the name of the river.

We arrived in Mongandjo at noon. The three boatmen returned to Basoko and we were left to go our separate ways. Father Mietek set off on his moped on a two-week tour of up-country villages and Victor took us firmly under his wing. He proposed that we hire a dug-out and two paddlers to take us the 18 miles to Yambuya and brought two men to meet us for this purpose: Marot, deputy headmaster of the village primary school (clearly 'moonlighting'), and Modjo, a fisherman. We negotiated a price and arranged to set out before dawn the next day.

In the meantime, we explored the village in the company of a young schoolteacher. Church, school, market, houses, a small commercial centre (operated by traders who came up from the Zaïre River once a week) were interspersed with plantations of coffee and oil palm. The traditional medicine man, the *mokibisi*,

Julie watches the boat crew prepare a meal during a stop on the way up the Aruwimi River.

Marot and Modjo arrived at Victor's house at 3.30 next morning and were surprised to find that we had slept with the window open. It had been a warm night, there had been few mosquitoes around and we were not worried about thieves, so to us it had seemed a natural thing to do, but an African closes his window at night to keep out evil spirits.

We were away by 4 am. Victor had decided that we needed looking after and would accompany us as far as Yambuya. Wicker chairs were placed in the dug-out for us and we sat regally one behind the other for our triumphal passage up the river. It was quiet and cool before dawn, the silence broken only by the harsh cries of leopards and the barking of baboons. As the sun rose, mist lifted in layers from the spectral forest on the river banks. An old man smoking fish over a charcoal fire in his *pirogue* smiled toothlessly and offered Victor a fish he had just caught. The sun got higher and hotter. The water hyacinth blooms opened, hornbills and toucans flapped noisily by, butterflies flitted silently from leaf to leaf and monkeys chattered loudly in the trees.

We kept close to the bank to avoid the strong current midstream. Marot, in the prow, poled, forcing the pole hard down against the bank, running three steps towards us, then retrieving the pole and starting all over again. Modjo, in the stern, paddled. Despite their exertions, they kept up a constant flow of conversation and laughter. Our proximity to the bank enabled us to get an eyeball-to-eyeball view of the caterpillars, grubs and dragonflies that carried out their business on the leaves and flowers, but the drawback was that we were prey constantly to the '*marangwa*', small black flies that swarmed out of the undergrowth and settled on any exposed flesh they could find. They didn't sting or irritate, but they did draw blood and by the end of the journey we were a mass of red blotches.

We covered only 1–2 miles per hour and with a mid-morning break didn't approach Yambuya until around 5 o'clock

showed us the array of potions and cures in his dispensary which he claimed were effective against evil spirits and enemies, and could mend broken bones and cure headaches, stomach aches and syphilis. The potions were made from animal and vegetable matter according to secret recipes passed down to him by his grandfather. His shop was as busy as a Western doctor's surgery and, as a concession to modernity, he wore a white shirt bearing a large red cross.

At a fishing camp on the Aru-wimi, John examines a shelter where fishermen rest during the heat of the day.

The wives of the chief at Yam-buya prepare manioc flour by pounding the dried root with a wooden pestle.

in the afternoon. We left the *pirogue* at the small fishing village of Kikole, a few miles downstream from Yambuya, as Marot and Modjo didn't want to chance the rapids that lay between the two. We marched through mixed deciduous and bamboo forest, arriving in what we thought was Yambuya around 6 pm, only to discover that the village was in fact Bamanga and that Yambuya was on the opposite bank. We realised our mistake: the natives of Yambuya had fled their village on Stanley's approach 100 years before and had established a new village on the other side of the river, while Stanley built his base camp on the site of the original village, where we now were. We were introduced to the *chef de localité* who, in the African tradition of hospitality, offered us a bed for the night, and to Albert, an old friend of Victor's who happened to be living in the village with his wife and family. Then Victor, conscientious to the last, sat us down to discuss what should happen to us next and to whom he should pass on the responsibility for our safe passage on the next leg of our journey to the town of Banalia.

He presented the options open to us: we could try to hire a *pirogue* and paddlers to take us on up the Aruwimi through numerous sets of rapids, but there was only one *pirogue* in the village big enough to handle white water and both it and its owner were away; we could walk to Banalia with a guide and porters, but this trek would take four to five days and no one was keen to accompany us because the few villages along the way were not very friendly; or we could walk to the village of N'gazi, 18 miles south of the Aruwimi, get a lift from there to Yan-gambi on the Zaïre River, from there to Kisangani, and finally to Banalia by the main road north, a journey it was reckoned would take about three days. We favoured the first two options as they followed the route taken by Stanley, but it was clear that we were in a minority of two. We gave in gracefully and opted for route three. It was arranged that next day Albert would take us on a tour of Yambuya and Liongo, the village at the third set of rapids, and that the following day he and a friend would guide us through the forest to N'gazi. Victor meticulously drew up a contract stating that we would pay Albert 600 zaïres for these services. This was signed by John and Albert, witnessed by Victor and then sealed with the official stamp of the Basoko Catholic Mission, which Victor produced from his pack.

We were surprised to find that Victor, Marot and Modjo intended to set off back to Mongandjo immediately to take advantage of the cool night air. We were exhausted after the 14-hour journey, having simply sat for most of the time, while they—or at least Marot and Modjo—had exerted themselves non-stop. We were sorry to see them go for they had been good friends to us over the last few days and we promised to write and send photos from England.

*****

On 15 June 1887 the expedition reached the first of the rapids and the end of navigation on the Aruwimi River. On the south bank lay the village of Yambuya, a place that was to become notorious not only to the expedition members but also to the outside world.

Deviation and Disaster

The story of the Rear Column starts on 16 June 1887 with Stanley's capture of the village of Yambuya and its conversion to a fortified camp. Barttelot arrived on 22 June after delivering Tippu Tip to Stanley Falls. Two days later the remaining river boats left Yambuya for Leopold-ville. The expedition was alone. Stanley lost no time in organising his advance party to march out into the unmapped forest, his aim to reach the besieged Emin Pasha as swiftly as possible. Behind him he would leave Barttelot and Jameson to guard the supplies, tend the sick and to follow on once the remaining expedition members and the extra men promised by Tippu Tip had arrived. He left detailed written instructions for the Major in which various options were outlined in the event that Tippu did not provide the

The expedition lands at Yambuya and takes the village by force.

full complement of porters required. A priority list of essential goods was drawn up, the possibility of multiple marches was touched on, and if all else failed, Barttelot was instructed to await his leader's return. After making initial contact with Emin and establishing the position in Equatoria, Stanley calculated he would be back in about five months, by October or November.

When Stanley marched away from Yambuya on 28 June 1887, he was accompanied by 383 men, four officers and his European servant, Hoffman. Under Barttelot's command were Jameson and 127 men, mostly sick. A further 128 men and three officers were awaited from down river. Losses in men had, by expedition standards, been small. Only 57 had either died or deserted since Matadi. A porter's life was not an enviable one. In addition to a 60 lb load he would be expected to carry a rifle, his personal kit and food—a total of about 80 lb weight—over difficult country, on meagre rations and often exposed to surprise attack. To compound these discomforts, he was subject to strict discipline, with floggings a regular occurrence and summary execution not unknown. There is no doubt that Stanley's fears of mass desertions on the part of his porters were well-founded.

Alone, the Major and Jameson got down to the business of fortifying the camp. Security was a major priority, as the goods they were guarding represented a veritable Aladdin's Cave, a tempting prize for native or Arab alike. The camp was completely enclosed by a wooden palisade guarded at night by sentries. The automatic penalty for a sentry found asleep on duty was 25 lashes with a barbaric whip known as a 'chicotte' and on most days the morning parade was followed by a flogging. The regular administration of this terrible punishment could have done nothing for the morale of the men.

Numerous attempts were made to open trading relations with the local natives who had set up a new village on the opposite bank of the Aruwimi. It was not long before Barttelot adopted the Arab ivory traders' method of doing business. This was simply to capture native women and children and then to ransom them back to their families in return for food. For a while this system brought in a few fish, chickens and the odd goat, but food was to be a constant problem, not least for the men, who had no share of what meat the officers could find or extort, and had to fend for themselves.

Barttelot appears to have been a man totally ill-equipped for life in a static camp. Unlike Jameson, who took a keen interest in his surroundings, sketching and collecting flora and fauna, Barttelot's sole preoccupation was with the running and discipline of the camp. His main leisure activity was reported as 'walking up and down'. He was a man with a quick and powerful temper and a well-documented loathing of the black man, attributes that did not augur well for the months of inactivity that lay ahead. Tippu Tip's promise of arriving with the extra men 'in nine days' had not materialised and no word had been received.

On 14 August 1887 the monotony of camp life was broken by the arrival of the *Stanley* with the remaining officers and men. The new arrivals' first impressions were good: 'A capital place for a camp,' wrote Rose Troup, an impression that was not to last. The Rear Column was now at full strength: the five officers, Barttelot, Jameson, Troup, Ward and Bonny, and 246 men. Seven men had died in camp since Stanley's departure. The pleasure of reunion was short-lived. Within days the bickering that was to become a feature of the officers' existence had started.

During August Arab activity in the area intensified and rumours abounded that either the porters or Stanley were about to appear at any moment. Jameson and Ward were dispatched on the overland route to Stanley Falls, where they arrived after a five- or six-day journey to be received by Tippu with great courtesy.

The officers of the Rear Column watch as Arabs plunder the village opposite their camp.

Foraging for food at Yambuya was rarely as successful as this picture suggests.

He explained that he had sent the promised porters by river, but that on the Aruwimi they had had to fight, had run out of powder and been forced to retreat. They were now scattered over the country and it would be difficult to get them together again. Jameson and Ward left with a promise that Tippu would do his best to deliver the men to their camp. In the meantime, he sent Selim Mohammed, his nephew, and a small band of men back with the two officers.

At Yambuya, Selim Mohammed set up camp next door, Ward fell ill and retired to bed for six weeks, and the rest dropped back into the gloom of powerless waiting. With Arabs active all over the area, trouble was constant. It was next to impossible to trade with the natives, food was an ever-increasing problem and desertions were starting. By October there was still no movement and it was the turn of Barttelot and Troup to trek to the Falls to nag Tippu. It was clear that the latter's real problem in gathering men stemmed from conditions in the Yambuya camp itself. Word had spread about the harsh discipline and lack of food and none of Tippu's men were willing to submit to this sort of indignity. Tippu had therefore sent to Kasongo, his base on the Lualaba River, for fresh men. Action was in hand, even if moving at the slow pace of African affairs. Barttelot and Troup returned to Yambuya to continue the vigil.

Christmas came and the officers had jam roly poly pudding, but none of the news that they longed for. The dark forest closed around them; they felt forgotten and abandoned by the world. More importantly, morale amongst the men was at a low ebb and they were dying off at an alarming rate. Forty men had been buried since Stanley's departure.

Jameson's diary entry for 31 December sums up the officers' feelings: 'The last six months have been the most miserable and useless I have ever spent anywhere, and goodness knows when it is going to end.'

In the New Year they started to go over all the options again, including the multiple marches suggested by Stanley. This plan would involve moving as many loads as could be carried to a certain point, returning for a second batch, and so on until all the goods had reached that point, then repeating the whole process again and again. Since they only had about 100 fit men, it would take years to reach Equatoria using this method. Troup, the experienced transport officer, recorded his view of the proposal: '[it] would have been in my opinion perfectly insane.' The idea was rejected as impractical.

By February the situation was going from bad to worse. Jameson was still bemoaning the turn of events: 'This waiting here in utter darkness is sickening, and the men are dying like rotten sheep.'

There were 51 graves now in the cemetery. On 9 February another was added. In a drastic effort to stop desertions, one of the Sudanese soldiers, who had deserted and had had the bad luck to be captured and returned by the Arabs, was sentenced to death and shot before the assembled company. It was time for another excursion to Stanley Falls.

On St Valentine's Day 1888 Barttelot and Jameson left for the Falls, only to discover that Tippu, who had gone to Kasongo himself to speed up recruiting, was still away and his date of return imminent, but unknown. They hung around for a month and then decided that, at last, positive action should be taken. Jameson was dispatched up river to Kasongo to chase up Tippu and pursue the improbable plan, hatched by the two officers, of hiring 1000 men and not just the 600 for whom they had waited so long.

Whilst Barttelot and Jameson were away, Rose Troup was left in command of the camp where the atmosphere was a

Tippu Tip's flotilla of canoes descending the Congo River.

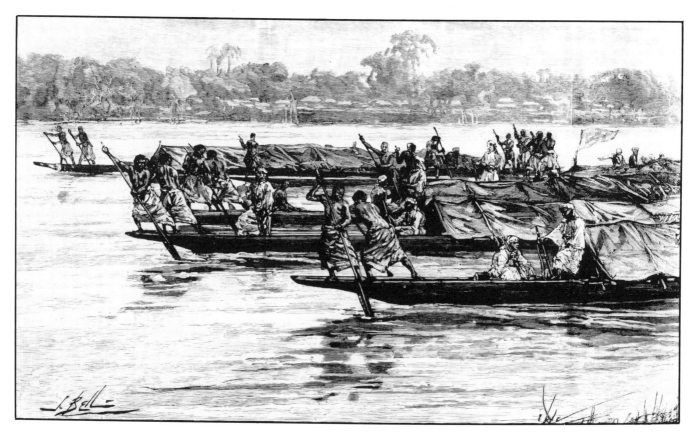

60

good deal more relaxed. Jameson, on the way to the Aruwimi, had noted in his diary that the European officers at the stations along the river were in the habit of keeping native wives. Troup and Ward were old Congo hands and soon improved their home comforts by the addition of slave girls bought from the Arabs. The old soldier, Bonny, followed suit. Unfortunately for the officers, this pleasant little arrangement ended after only a few days when the girls escaped and were not seen again.

The break from the rigour of Major Barttelot's rule lasted only about five weeks. On 24 March he staggered back into camp, suffering from sickness and loss of weight. He thought that the Arabs at the Falls had poisoned him. The officers were surprised to learn of Jameson's mission to Kasongo and even more surprised when they heard the Major's latest idea. This was to send a telegram to the expedition's organising committee in London to advise them of the situation and to request their consent for his proposed actions. The nearest telegraph office was a mere 1500 miles away on the Atlantic coast. Ward was asked to run down to the post office. Both Ward and Troup considered this a dangerous and pointless exercise, since there was nothing the committee could say other than that Barttelot should proceed as per Stanley's instructions. Argument became pointless when Barttelot got wind of the goings on during his absence from the camp. Both men were starting to have doubts about Barttelot's sanity. But, glad to be out of the way, Ward set off overland to the Congo River with Troup as escort. In their absence more petty disputes with the Arab camp next to the fort soon had Barttelot rushing off down the familiar road to Stanley Falls, intent on having Selim Mohammed recalled.

Rose Troup, having seen Ward off, spent some time trying to buy goats for the camp. On his way back to Yambuya, he was surprised to bump into Barttelot returning along the busy Falls road. The two men were on less than friendly terms and were not overjoyed to see one another. Troup recorded that the Major looked 'terribly ill and very disturbed', and Barttelot's view of Troup was 'sick as usual, and with no goats'. They had time enough to have a row about Troup's conduct whilst in command of the camp before the Major rushed on to see what latest disaster had overtaken the Rear Column in his absence. Troup managed to fall over a log and injure his leg, limping into camp a day later.

The Major relieved him of his responsibility for the stores, and together they spent a week making a complete inventory of all that remained. Troup then retired to his hut to nurse his injuries, which had got much worse. Barttelot and Bonny were left alone to feed off each other's prejudices and fantasies. It is worth noting that Stanley later discovered that Bonny was an opium addict who, with free access to the medical supplies, had been indulging his addiction all along.

April was passing and nothing constructive had happened. There was no word from Tippu or Jameson. Troup was confined to his hut and Ward was making his way to the coast. Neither of these two would play any further part in the main events of the expedition. The arrival of the Free State steamer, *A.I.A.*, on 8 May provided a break in camp routine. Lieutenant van Kerckhoven was aboard and had come to return Ward's escort who had been left at Bangala. The Belgian had been surprised to learn that they were still at Yambuya, assuming that they had all moved on months before. Troup had developed a large tumour and could not leave his bed. The engineer from the boat thought he looked 'as if he had not a week to live'. The steamer left on 11 May for Stanley Falls, taking with it 1500 lb of ivory from the Arab camp as a service for Tippu. A few days later a firm rumour reached Yambuya that Tippu Tip and Jameson had returned to the Falls. Barttelot was off again, rushing down to the Congo in time to catch up with the

steamer, then on in comfort to Stanley Falls. The party from Kasongo had not arrived, but were expected any day.

On the evening of 22 May the flotilla of canoes arrived. Barttelot was overjoyed to see Jameson, the only man he felt he could trust, and was not slow to pour out all his troubles to him. The next day they got down to business. Tippu Tip had promised Jameson 800 men, and it was known that this many, and more, were now available, but when Barttelot broached the subject he was told that the maximum number he could have was 400. It seemed that Tippu had had every intention of providing more men, until the real purpose of van Kerckhoven's visit was revealed. The Belgian proposed that Tippu should take possession for the State of the land north of the Congo up to the Ubangi River. The Free State officers had never been in favour of Tippu's appointment as governor, believing that his real intention was to move west down the Congo River and force them

out. By deflecting his attention to the north they hoped to forestall this move and give themselves time to occupy the area up to Stanley Falls. This proposal had attractions for Tippu, but he could also see the underlying reasoning. He decided it would be wise to hold more men in reserve.

Having completed their business, Barttelot and Jameson set off to prepare for departure from Yambuya, accompanied by the new Arab headman, Muni Somai, hired for the extravagant fee of £1000. Back at camp they started on the mammoth task of reducing the loads from the standard weight of 60 lb to 40 lb, in line with a clause in the agreement made with Tippu Tip for the supply of these new men. On 4 June two steamers arrived, the *Stanley* and the *A.I.A.*, the former bringing Tippu's long-awaited Belgian assistant to his post, the latter carrying Tippu himself. This was his first visit to the camp and, to the officers, he must have been a welcome sight. After all the broken promises, his presence seemed to confirm that this time it was all real. On 9 June the steamers left and with them went the desperately sick John Rose Troup and the interpreter Assad Farran who was being sent home as useless. Assad would soon reap his revenge.

At last all was ready and on Monday 11 June 1888, almost a year after arriving at Yambuya, the Rear Column marched out following Stanley's trail. Those left behind at Yambuya—the dead, the sick and the deserters—amounted to 108. The column now numbered over 700 people. The roll call was:

Zanzibari porters	115
Sudanese soldiers	22
Somalis	1
Tippu's natives	430
Camp followers	150
Arab headman	1
Officers	3
Total	722

*****

Bamanga (ex-Yambuya) was, when we visited it in 1986, a small village of thatched huts set in compounds around a large open area of flat brown earth, cleared of vegetation to reduce cover for snakes and breeding areas for mosquitoes. The village was not on a road. Its only contacts with the outside world were via the river and the forest track to N'gazi. On the night of our arrival, 99 years almost to the day after Stanley, a ritual mourning ceremony was taking place. The younger brother of the traditional chief had just died and the villagers were undergoing seven days of mourning. Fires burned in a large circle around a central fire where two drummers sat. Women with white clay daubed on their foreheads circled round this central fire, stamping their feet and swinging their hips. One of the drummers started up a chant, beating out the complex rhythm on a tall standing drum while his companion marked time on two smaller drums suspended on a pole. The dead man had been found lying on the floor of his hut one morning. It was not clear whether he had died of natural causes or through foul play. To be on the safe side, one of the chants was aimed at any culprit there might be: 'If you are the murderer, may you know no rest' (it sounded more impressive in the local language!). We were told by our new guardian and guide, Albert, that there were over 400 traditional songs and chants for events that mark the passage of life, such as birth, circumcision, marriage and death.

Next morning, after we had spent a stifling night on a hard wooden bedstead in the chief's airless house, Albert took us in a small dug-out to the headland above Bamanga at the start of the main rapids. It was completely choked with bush, creepers and trees and was impenetrable. It was as though Stanley's base camp at Yambuya had never existed. In the African forest a year is a long time; in 100 years the forest had totally reclaimed its own, leaving not a single trace of the men who had spent so many frustrating months there, or of the graves of those who had never left. Just as disappointing was the villagers' ignorance of Stanley and the Rear Column. There seemed to be no one, even among the elderly, who knew of the white men's fortified camp there and the strangers from Zanzibar, Sudan and Somaliland who had accompanied the Europeans. This we could only attribute to the decimation of the population during the Congo Free State era when whole villages were captured, killed or fled before the onslaught of Arab slave raiders. No doubt the ancestors of the present inhabitants of Yambuya and Bamanga had settled in the area long after the original inhabitants had been dispersed and the danger from the Arabs was past.

We sat on the rocks at the water's edge and watched a fisherman fixing the conical wicker basket he used to trap fish. The rapids here produced back-waves of three feet in places and fish that were swept into the traps by the force of water were unable to escape. We then paddled across the river to the new Yambuya in preparation for the trek to Liongo, which Albert told us was just three miles up river. This seemed a gentle stroll, until we realised that Albert's idea of three miles was vastly different from our own. The 'gentle stroll' took us three hours of hard effort, fighting our way along a narrow, densely overgrown track where branches and creepers had to be cut away with machetes. But first there was Yambuya itself. The village was strung out along the river bank, divided into several sub-sections, or *localités*, each of which had its own petty chief whom courtesy required that we greet, explain ourselves to, and take photographs of. It was 30 June, Independence Day and a public holiday, and there seemed to be considerable evidence, even at a relatively early hour of the morning, of the influence of *lutuku*, the locally produced spirit, on the populace.

We passed the second cataract, Iyole, and finally reached Liongo, the village situated at the third. The rapids here extended much further than those at Yambuya. We began to see why the villagers had not been keen to transport us through the seven sets of rapids that separated Yambuya from Banalia. The village was neatly laid out around an open space with, rather unusually, a small shrub garden in the centre. Between the huts were garden plots growing tomatoes, onions and maize. In the *baraza*, the open-sided men's meeting hut, the village males relaxed in woven reed deck chairs. As a white woman in African villages, I was always treated as an honorary man, so on this occasion was invited to enter the *baraza* with Albert and John. The local protestant pastor (of the Kimbanguist Church, an indigenous Christian sect) asserted his authority by asking to see the permits for our journey through Zaïre. Once he had inspected our visas and come to the conclusion that we were not dangerous, just crazy, he was

very friendly and everyone settled down to smoke John's cigarettes and discuss our route.

The people seemed to live well here; there was plenty of fish in the river, the gardens produced good crops, and the forest was full of game—monkey, wild pig, antelope, elephant and buffalo. This was in marked contrast to the situation that Jameson had found 100 years before, when he had vainly scoured the surrounding forest with his hunting rifle. It

The track through the forest from Yambuya to N'gazi crossed many streams and small rivers.

was no doubt another indication of the effects of the de-population of the area following that period.

That evening a group of patients gathered, to whom we were expected to dispense cures and advice. The villagers were sure that as Europeans, with access to wonder-drugs, we had the means at our disposal to treat their various ailments. This was always the case, we had found, in countries like Zaïre with little or no health care in remote areas. With an adequate knowledge of first aid, but with no medical training, we did what we could and trusted that our remedies had no harmful effects. Vitamin pills were always our standby if we were unsure how to treat the complaint. They were brightly coloured, attractive panaceas, which, although they wouldn't cure the ill, might do some good and certainly wouldn't do any harm.

When surgery hour was over, Albert suggested that a drink might be in order. We should buy some beer and *lutuku*.
'Where does the beer come from?' I asked.
'From N'gazi. My sister's husband goes twice a week. He takes two crates of empties and brings back full ones.'
Walking 18 miles with two crates and 20 large bottles of beer on one's back sounded punishing, but on reflection we realised that it probably represented a smaller load than that carried by one of Stanley's porters. Little wonder that so few of them survived the experience. We handed over the money and Albert set off to track down his sister's husband. On his return we stuck to beer, but Albert and the chief downed quantities of the potent home-made *lutuku*, to obvious effect.

Next morning we were up early in readiness for the day's march, but Albert seemed to have trouble in leaving his bed. Finally, after much prompting, he and his number two were ready to go, our rucksacks slung from rattan bands around their foreheads, the traditional method of carrying heavy objects in Africa. We thanked the chief for his hospitality, distributed presents of money, soap powder and soap to him and his wives and mother, and set out through the forest.

Although unable to follow Stanley's route to Banalia at this point, we were following closely in Barttelot's footsteps on the first leg of his many journeys to the Stanley Falls station. The going was easy at first, the forest cool and damp, the path clear and wide, but this did not last long. Soon knobbly roots were tripping us up and columns of ants investigating our clothing. Albert and Djodjo ran lightly ahead with our heavy packs while we lumbered slowly behind. We would find them waiting for us in a clearing, ready to set off again the moment we appeared. When we stopped to rest, the forest surrounded us with sound. It was never silent. We heard bird calls, grasshoppers, the creaking of branches, the occasional patter of rain in the tops of the tallest trees, rustlings in the dense undergrowth and distant crashes as monkeys leapt from branch to branch. Dragonflies, praying mantis and centipedes we saw in abundance, but of larger animals we saw nothing. Our noisy progress had no doubt driven them away, and even if they had been standing close to the path, the creepers and undergrowth were so thick that we probably wouldn't have been aware of them.

In the afternoon a string of villagers passed us on their way back from N'Gazi where they had been selling fish and produce in the market. They laughed at our slow progress; Europeans were such feeble physical specimens. We had got used to Africans finding us objects of amusement; this we did not mind. What did disturb us was that there was clearly a long way still to go, and we had already been walking for seven hours. Our hearts sank, but there was nothing to be done except press on. We had already forded nine streams and Albert assured us that there was only one more to go. Some of them had been pretty little rivulets with clear water running shallowly over golden sand, while others had been knee-deep and murky. I took off my boots to cross as I didn't like squelching along with boots full of water. Luckily there didn't seem to be any leeches here. John always kept his boots on to cross rivers, insisting this was the safer and more sensible way to do it. I tried not to look smug when the wet sand that got into his boots caused painful blisters.

Albert had saved the best river for last. He and Djodjo were well ahead as usual when we came to the bank. John strode into the water, only to disappear up to his arm pits. Forewarned, I took off my trousers and gingerly tried a different route. I had more luck and submerged only to the knicker line, but had to plough through soft oozy matter that raised unpleasant brown clouds on the surface. Well, at least that was over. I put on my boots for the last time, and shortly afterwards, around 5 pm, we left the forest and entered the regimented ranks of a rubber plantation. A further hour's walk through the lines of rubber trees brought us to a large group of scattered buildings—houses, offices, a factory, warehouses—which a sign board informed us was INERA-N'gazi, the N'gazi section of the *Institut National de Recherche Agronomique*. Albert took us to the house of the *Chef de Station*, the director, who he assured us had transport and would be able to get us to Yangambi. Nkangolo Muamba Dipu was most welcoming, once he had got over his surprise at two Europeans suddenly appearing out of the bush, and installed us in one of the Institute's empty guest houses.

Next morning he explained to us that the only vehicle in working order was the tractor which paid a weekly visit to Yangambi on Fridays (it was now Wednesday). We were welcome to travel with it if we wished. From Yangambi we should be able to get a lift in one of the lorries that passed through on Sundays heading for the market at Kisangani. We accepted his offer gratefully. This leg of the journey was clearly going to take considerably

longer than the three days Victor had posited, but time in Africa is a more flexible element than in the developed world and one has to adapt to local conditions.

We discovered that our guest house doubled up as the executive canteen. The cook arrived early, stoked up a fire in the blackened brick cook house and proceeded to feed substantial meals to the white-collar employees who ate either in 'our' dining room or out on the verandah, according to rank.

The director's assistant, Bosulu N'ginda, came after work to give us a guided tour of INERA. We assumed this would take in the factory and warehouses in the compound, but found instead that we were to make an eight-mile walking tour of the plantation and workers' village. John groaned and hobbled along on his blistered feet. If nothing else, we would certainly be fit at the end of this expedition. Our guide pointed out the identification marks and the cuts on the trunks of the rubber trees and explained the method of exploitation. Latex collected from the plantation was treated with acid in the factory, driven in the trailer to Yangambi, then shipped downriver to Kinshasa. However, since the collapse in world rubber prices, they were doing very little business and only survived because they were a part of the national university. Most other plantations in northern Zaïre had long since been abandoned. Where the rubber trees stopped, the workers' village began. The Belgians, who had built the station in the late 1940s when independence for the Congo must have seemed inconceivable, did not believe in having their workers billeted too close to their own quarters. The houses, now a little dilapidated, were of a solid brick construction, built in pairs along straight quasi-suburban roads. There was a dispensary, a market and even a group of houses for retired employees.

Beyond the INERA township lay the native village of Turumbu where we met the Catholic pastor to whom we had a letter of introduction from our assiduous friend, Victor. He lived with his wife and 12 children in a crumbling old colonial house with a verandah approached by a wide flight of steps, next door to the large church, another legacy of colonial times. He showed us with pride the church's vaulted brick architecture and brightly painted alcoves, its statues, and the traditional drums used to provide music for the services. He spoke of the Africanisation of the Church in Zaïre, the lack of doctors and medicines in the villages and the local Catholic 'Légionnaires' whose function was to meet for prayer and to help the sick and needy. When we left, his wife generously gave us four eggs, a rare treat. In return we gave the pastor a coloured picture guide to Britain. Almost any meeting in Africa has to involve the exchange of gifts of a similar value. It would be insulting to give your host a present of a lesser value than the one he has offered. The most valued gift is something that is unobtainable locally, not necessarily an expensive item. We found that a post card showing the queen on horseback was particularly popular, bringing forth gasps of wonder and astonishment.

At 6.45 next morning there was an urgent knock at the door. It was Bosulu who informed us that the tractor was about to set off for Yangambi. We had expected to leave at 8 o'clock. By now we had rucksack packing down to a fine art and, despite this trick, were ready to leave within 15 minutes. We said our final thanks and goodbyes to the director and his staff and climbed up into the trailer to take our places on the two wicker chairs that had been provided for us. Once again it was to be a regal procession.

Our courtiers consisted of INERA employees who squatted on oil drums or perched on the edge of the trailer during the bumpy ride along the forest track. Overhanging branches showered us all with water and villagers waved as we passed. Some attempted to jump on to the slow-moving vehicle for a free ride, but were firmly repulsed by two men who came along for that express purpose. On the outskirts of Yangambi we passed several INERA coffee and cocoa plantations and experimental rice paddies before the tractor driver dropped us at the Catholic mission of Notre-Dame, telling us there were two Polish priests there who would make us welcome. Just as a white person assumes that two Africans will automatically be bosom friends, despite different geographical and tribal origins, so Africans always assume that whites in Africa are blood brothers. We hoped that the two Poles would feel the same way about us.

Having arrived rather early, we did not get to meet the two Fathers for some hours. Neither were at home and returned only at lunch time. Meanwhile we sat outside, providing endless opportunities for the youngsters who gathered in droves around us from the mission school, the Ecole de St Jean, to practise their English. As they all seemed to be on the same lesson, what started out as fun soon became somewhat repetitious. Father Josef's arrival thankfully put a stop to English classes. He hospitably gave us lunch, and then drove us down to the town's crumbling commercial centre where he thought we should find transport.

A local shopkeeper put two upright wooden chairs at our disposal and we sat at the edge of the dusty road feeling not a little conspicuous. His was the only shop open and sold only tinned sardines and condensed milk. The other shops, behind locked double doors on shady verandahs, were long abandoned as was the derelict hotel opposite, and hardly a soul stirred during the hot afternoon. The only trucks we saw were one that was practically rusted to the spot and another that passed us from time to time as it went around town touting for business for the morrow. It seemed we were out of luck; nothing moved on the 'highway' to

Kisangani. At about 6 o'clock, by which time we too had begun to feel rusted to the spot, Father Josef drove up in his Landrover to see if we were still there. He offered us overnight accommodation at the mission which we gratefully accepted. Yangambi had an even bigger mission compound than Basoko and in its heyday had been home to many resident and visiting priests. Now there was just Father Josef, Father Georges and occasional itinerant Fathers, Brothers and seminarists. The mission stations of Zaïre are, or rather were, little oases of rest, comfort and good food for the European traveller. The reluctance of priests to take on missionary work and the increase in the number of travellers who have abused their hospitality mean that fewer and fewer missions now open their doors to passing guests. We had a great deal of respect for the Catholic Fathers. Whatever one might think of the work they tried to do, one could not but admire their commitment. Unlike Protestant missionaries who normally worked on the basis of a short-term contract and moved on after three years or so, the Catholics were prepared to commit their whole lives to a single mission. Although not of the faith, we did at least provide a listening ear for Father Josef that evening. New people to talk to didn't come his way every day.

At 6.15 next morning Father Georges, on his way to conduct a Mass in a nearby village, dropped us once again in the commercial centre, and again the shopkeeper offered us two chairs to sit on. We were becoming part of the landscape. The lorry which had promised departure for today showed no sign of fulfilling this promise, and the few other vehicles we saw were not destined for Kisangani. At least there was more going on today. It was Saturday and salongo day. Salongo is the Zaïrean version of an idea borrowed by President Mobutu from the Chinese: every worker should donate some time on his day off to community work, which generally consists of clearing under-growth, roadsides and drainage ditches. Officials of Zaïre's one political party, the *Mouvement Populaire de la Révolution*, were responsible for organising salongo groups, and just opposite us the local commander in his smart white safari suit and white wellington boots was directing the operations of a band of men armed with machetes who were clearing the undergrowth from the side of the road. Other groups passed, machetes in hand, on their way to do their civic duty. The last time we had seen salongo in action in Zaïre was 12 years previously. It was an impressive achievement that it was still operating.

Late in the morning Father Josef came by in the Landrover and suggested we would do better down at the 'beach', the riverside dock area. We were happy to agree as our prospects at the commercial centre were less than rosy. He dropped us off there and we said goodbye for the third time, taking up residence in the shade of an abandoned warehouse. The drawback to our new position was the presence of the only 'down and out' I have ever seen in Zaïre, a middle-aged man, with wild matted hair, dressed in a shabby European-style suit who, very politely, asked for a cigarette. On being given one, he backed away obsequiously while the local children jeered and threw stones.

We lunched off *mikati*—fried dough balls—with peanut paste from a stall nearby. Various vehicles passed, but none were going out of town. The hours ticked slowly by and we were beginning to wonder if the priests at the mission would let us stay another night when a cloud of dust in the distance announced the approach of a vehicle. We stepped out into the road and waved frantically. A green Landrover pick-up screeched to a halt in front of us and who should jump out but Monteiro, our saviour from Basoko. Were we glad to see him! When we had all got over our surprise and explanations (he was going to Kisangani on business for four days) he

loaded our gear into the back and we climbed into the cab. The road clung closely to the river, passing through villages of thatched huts. Men lay in wicker deck chairs in the shade and children played with trucks ingeniously made from bent wire and sticks, fishing nets spread around them on the ground to dry. The children gaped and waved as we passed while scrawny hens fled from under our wheels.

As Monteiro was going down with malaria, John offered to drive, a suggestion the half-dozen employees perched in the open back of the Landrover did not altogether appreciate. It requires skill to drive over deeply rutted and pot-holed dirt roads. John was a little out of practice and, he claimed, the brakes on the vehicle were far from adequate. It was a rough ride for the three of us in the cab as our heads regularly came up to meet the roof, but it must have been much more bruising for the men in the back. Luckily the road improved once we had crossed the Lindi River on the Simi-Simi ferry. The ferry boat was German-built, donated by the Federal Republic in 1979. It chugged slowly across the river on its one working engine, the other having broken down some years earlier. The perennial problem of Zaïre, as of most Third World countries, is the non-availability of spare parts and the scarcity of skilled labour to repair and replace. Having said that, I should add that a Zaïrean mechanic can often patch up an engine or piece of machinery that in the developed world would long ago have been relegated to the scrap heap. The sunset over the dark, deep Lindi flowing between palm- and forest-clad banks cast a blood-red glow which quickly faded as the tropical night descended, duskless.

The graded road on the opposite bank was a joy to aching bones. We rattled along and soon entered the outskirts of Kisangani. Our mouths fell open in amazement as tarmac roads, street lights, large town houses, buses, university buildings and even a set of traffic lights (non-operational) hove into view. These adjuncts of civilisation belonged to a different world from the one we had grown used to. Monteiro, now back in the driving seat, was as punch-drunk as we were. The Landrover careered from one side of the road to the other as we exclaimed over yet another urban phenomenon we had forgotten existed. Angry hoots from other drivers reminded him that here he had to keep to his own side of the road. We were three country cousins, out of our depth in the big city.

Monteiro dropped us at the Hotel Olympia and promised to be our guest for dinner one evening, then drove off to find the friend with whom he was to stay. The hotel was Greek-run and well-known amongst the overland fraternity for whom Kisangani is on one of the major north-south routes through Africa. A large four-wheel drive vehicle was parked in the compound, en route for Kenya, and three German boys were tinkering with bits of engine. After dinner in the open-air restaurant we got into conversation with a Danish couple, Finn and Jytte, who, with their two young daughters, were taking the overland route home after a three-year contract in Kenya. They had spent a few days in Kisangani as a rest from the road, giving the two girls endless opportunities to drink Coca-Cola, and were planning to leave on Monday, the day after next, heading north for Banalia, the very place we had been trying so hard to reach. We had to change a traveller's cheque at a bank on Monday so weren't in a position to beg a lift from them! It was Saturday night and the Greek customers at the bar were celebrating. Tired by our long day,

we were asleep by 11 o'clock, only to be rudely awakened at 2.30 am when the Greeks ended their party with a nostalgic burst of traditional plate-smashing.

Washing was my first priority as clothes were running out and I soon filled the communal washing line with all the clothes we possessed. Sunday was a quiet day. After our experiences in Kinshasa, a Sunday afternoon stroll around the streets held no attractions. Instead we read, caught up on our diaries and played with the two dwarf chimpanzees, mother and baby, who lived in the hotel compound along with a parrot and half a dozen scrawny cats who silently padded under the tables in the evening hoping for crumbs to fall from above.

Next morning we said goodbye to Finn, Jytte and the girls who were setting off north, then walked into the town centre. The last time we had been in Kisangani was 12 years before when the town had had a certain rough air of prosperity about it. Now we were dismayed to see how shabby it had grown. Many of the shops and offices were closed and semi-derelict, including the large supermarket we remembered. There were several small shops open, but their range of goods was limited and their prices high. Twelve years earlier, President Mobutu's edict that all foreign traders must leave Zaïre had not had time to take full effect and businesses were still operating. In the intervening years shops and enterprises had been Africanised, often with devastating results. The new traders did not have their European predecessors' connections and were unable to replenish stocks, many had no experience of running a trading concern and were thrown in at the deep end, in some cases corruption at the top had creamed off what profits there were, and then there were the effects of the extended family system, by which a wealthy man is expected to support his poorer relatives. It is an excellent social system in the village context, but in business terms it means that any profits there might be are never ploughed back into the enterprise and failure is not far away.

After a fairly conservative one and a half hours spent changing money in the *Banque de Zaïre*, we were back at the Olympia, making a bottle of beer last a long time while we pondered our next move, when we were surprised to see Finn and his daughters reappear. There was no sign of Jytte or their Landrover. Finn was phlegmatic about his tale of woe.

'We went to fill up before leaving and the man put diesel in the tank. It's a petrol engine. I'd already paid for the fuel before I realised what he'd done. They've emptied it out and refilled the tank with petrol but they won't let me take the vehicle away without paying for the petrol. I haven't got enough cash and now the banks are closed, so the garage has impounded the Landrover. Jytte's stayed with it to make sure nothing's stolen, whilst I try to raise the money.'

Luckily, having just been to the bank, we were able to lend Finn enough zaïres to return to the garage and bail out his vehicle and his wife. They drove back into the compound later that afternoon, poorer but otherwise none the worse for the experience, and determined to make another attempt at departure next morning.

Sorry as we were about their bad luck, we could not help but be pleased about its repercussions for us when Finn offered us a lift all the way to Banalia. We had done everything we needed to do in Kisangani, and were ready to get back to the Aruwimi River and Stanley's trail. The Rear Column's attempt to reach Banalia was much more of a struggle.

*****

From the outset, the march of the Rear Column was a shambles. There were too few officers to organise matters and the native porters supplied by Tippu Tip were out of control. It was part of the contract with Tippu that the European officers would have no authority over his men, who had refused to come if they were subject to the severe discipline that had prevailed at Yambuya. The headman, Muni Somai, proved to have next to no influence over the men, the result being that they did exactly as they pleased. They would march for a day or two and then rest up or collect food until they felt like moving on. Barttelot and Bonny had gone on ahead with their Zanzibaris whilst Jameson stayed in the rear, trying to encourage Muni to move his men on. The Zanzibaris had little more enthusiasm for the march and within four days 14 men had deserted with some of the most valuable loads. Jameson was ordered back to Yambuya to head them off. It is an indication of how slowly the march was progressing that Jameson covered the distance from Yambuya back to Muni and his men in less than a day. It had taken the column six days to reach that point. By 23 June the number of desertions had risen to 22, nearly 20 per cent of the Zanzibari force. Barttelot took drastic action, first confiscating all his men's guns and second, taking the extraordinary decision to put them in chains. Not actually having any fetters, he rushed off to Stanley Falls, 200 miles away, to get some from Tippu. Bonny was left in charge with orders to continue the march to a place called Banalya. Jameson, well in the rear, knew nothing about these goings on and was therefore unable to prevent them.

Tippu was surprised, not to say appalled, to see the Major yet again. He must have thought that he had removed this thorn in his side for ever. Pressed by Barttelot for more men, he wrote out instructions for an extra 60 men to be procured at Banalya, loaded up the Major with chains and sent him on his way.

When Barttelot reached Banalya on 17 July, Bonny had been there for two days with the advance column. Jameson was still struggling manfully in the rear, about five days behind. On receiving the requisition for men, Abdullah, the chief Arab at Banalya, refused to supply them, claiming that he simply did not have any to spare. This could not have helped Barttelot's already troubled state of mind. To make things worse, he had been given a copy of a statement made by the sacked interpreter, Assad Farran, to the Free State officers accusing him of brutality and, more seriously, claiming that Jameson had shot natives and taken part in a cannibal feast whilst travelling from Kasongo. The Major seems to have taken leave of his senses. He planned yet another trip to the Falls, this time ordering Abdullah to go with him to explain his refusal to supply men. Bonny records that Barttelot had thrown a knife at his ten-year-old servant, had bitten a woman on the cheek and was knocking the men about. He commented, 'I begin to think he is half-mad.'

Early on the morning of 19 July, Major Barttelot was disturbed by drumming and singing in the camp. When his orders for the noise to cease were ignored, he rushed out of his hut, revolver in hand. Finding a woman drumming, he kicked and threatened her. A shot rang out from behind a hut and Edmund Musgrave Barttelot fell to the ground stone dead.

For a few hours chaos reigned. Bonny did what he could to restore some sort of order, and over the next day or two managed to recover a fair number of the loads that disappeared. By the time Jameson appeared on the scene on 22 July, Bonny had buried the Major and all was quiet. Two days were spent recovering further loads and making an inventory, and on 25 July Jameson set off for Stanley Falls to take the tidings to Tippu Tip. On the road he learnt that the news had already reached the Falls and that Tippu Tip had acted with unusual speed. The murderer, a man named Sanga, husband of the woman beaten by Barttelot, had been caught and check-points set up along the Falls road to catch deserters and recover the expedition's goods. Over the next few days the Arab headman, Muni Somai, was found to be at fault, his contract torn up and he was obliged to return what he

had already been paid. Sanga was tried by the Belgians and Tippu, found guilty and sentenced to death.

Now Jameson could turn his attention to the business of getting the expedition under way again. What he needed was a good reliable Arab to lead the men. There were only three men who fitted the bill. One was in Kasongo, one refused to go and the last was Tippu Tip himself. Tippu had grave doubts about even letting Jameson return to his people at Banalya, saying to him, 'I am almost afraid to send you with these men; I think Major Barttelot's murder must have been a thing thought of by many.' Eventually, in exasperation at this whole mess, he did

Major Edmund Musgrave Barttelot died of a gunshot wound on 19 July 1888 at Banalya.

*James Jameson died of fever on
17 August 1888 at Bangala.*

offer to go himself, but on such terms that
it was impossible to accept. He would
guarantee nothing, but would require a
fee of £20,000 whatever the outcome.

Jameson had heard that Ward was at
the Bangala Station with the committee's
response to Barttelot's telegram. He now
decided to travel down river to discover
the instructions and possibly send a
further telegram to appraise the committee of the latest position. Jameson left
Stanley Falls by canoe on 9 August 1888,
and embarked on his last journey. He
developed a fever, arrived at Bangala in
a semi-coma on 16 August and died in
Ward's arms on the 17th. On that same
day at Banalya, on the Aruwimi River,
H M Stanley marched into camp to be
met by Bonny and the pathetic remnants
of the disaster called the Rear Column.

Ituri Forest

On 28 June 1887 Stanley was ready to lead the Advance Column out of Yambuya. The trumpets blew, the drums played and flags flew at the head of each company as the columns of porters filed out of the clearing by the Aruwimi River and plunged into unknown forest. Stanley stood at the gate of the fortified camp, reviewing the proud 400 marching to the relief of Equatoria. Next to him stood Major Barttelot and James Jameson, the men destined to command and bring up the Rear Column. As the last of the porters marched away, Stanley turned to make his farewells.

'Now, Major, my dear fellow, we are in for it. Neck or nothing! Remember your promise and we shall meet before many months.'

'I vow to goodness. I shall be after you sharp. Let me once get those fellows from Bolobo and nothing shall stop me,' were the Major's brave parting words. He little expected that the neck in question would be his. Stanley turned briskly away to take up his position at the head of the march.

The area that they were entering was certainly one of the darkest corners of the dark continent. All that was known was the position of Yambuya and that of Lake Albert at the southern limit of Equatoria, a straight-line distance calculated by Stanley at about 380 miles. What lay between these two points was completely unknown territory. Stanley and his officers would be the first Europeans ever to penetrate the murky depths of the vast Ituri Forest. On the basis of past experience, it was estimated that the 380-mile straight line would become a 550-mile line of march, a distance it was expected could be covered by the end of September 1887, a little over three months.

*****

Stanley arrived at Banalya, just over 90 miles up river from Yambuya, on 12 July after a march of fifteen days. A hundred years later and we managed to better his time by only one day, arriving at the same point after exactly two weeks. On leaving Kisangani with Finn and Jytte, we had crossed two major rivers in quick succession, the Tshopo and the Lindi, and then made good progress along a fairly reasonable road. This seemed to be a region of plenty. Along the route there was an abundance of goods for sale, huge pineapples, bananas, tomatoes, charcoal for cooking packed in long woven open-work baskets, just the right size to make a maximum bicycle load. In this relatively densely populated stretch of country, the big old trees had gone, to be replaced by secondary forest and bush, palms, bamboo, coffee bushes, all intersected by

Stanley gives Major Barttelot final instructions before leaving the Rear Column to its fate.

74

numerous small rivers. Finn and Jytte's elder daughter, 10-year-old Gina, a little blasé about African travel by now, had developed a passion for Enid Blyton and read her way through a Famous Five and a Secret Seven adventure during the five-hour drive. She and her sister, Mie, were destined to be stars of the English class when they reached home and settled into a Danish school.

For the princely sum of £1.50 per night, Banalia's Hotel Aruwimi provided us with a big, dark, airless room (the shutters would not open), an oil lamp, and a double bed with mattress and sheet. The proprietor and his numerous young female relatives were at first dumbfounded that two Europeans should want to stay in their establishment, but soon recovered sufficiently to find it uproariously funny. It was nice to know that we had not lost our knack of making people laugh! The hotel, like the town, had once been elegant. There was a large public room fronting the Aruwimi River, and what had once been a European-style bathroom. The chipped china was still in place, but now a large drum of water stood in the corner, with a ladle for flushing the toilet and showering. At least that was the theory. Whenever we went to the bathroom, it seemed that everyone and his dog had got there before us. The floor was wet, indicating the existence of water, but in the bottom of the barrel was half an inch which we couldn't even scoop up with the ladle.

The old colonial town was built along the river front where palm trees waved gracefully. Shops and villas with wide shady verandahs, now sadly dilapidated, lined the broad main street. At the end of this road, near the market and an incongruous roundabout, was the reason for the town's existence, the ferry crossing providing one of the many precarious

The Aruwimi Hotel at Banalia, our 'luxury' accommodation during a frustrating stay in the town.

links in the main road route north through Zaïre and eventually into the Central African Republic.

As we strolled by the river under a slim crescent moon, the romance of the evening was rudely dispelled by the arrival of a lorry that spewed forth dozens of passengers. With a tremendous volume of noise, they flocked up the steps of the hotel, laid claim to a piece of floor, wrapped themselves in lengths of cloth and lay down to sleep. We picked our way over the bodies to the dark sanctuary of our room, reflecting on the chances of finding any water in the bathroom.

Next morning, with equal commotion, the whole gang rose and climbed back on the lorry to await the first ferry of the day. We could see why the hotel was run down if its guests all slept on the floor free of charge. We followed them up the road, watched the ferry load up with several vehicles and a host of foot passengers, and said goodbye to our Danish friends who were continuing on the next stage of their journey to Europe. The ferry chugged away across the river and we turned our attention to the next leg of our own journey.

Our plan was to continue up the Aruwimi, as Stanley and the Advance Column had done, past Panga Falls and on to Bomili, before striking off across country towards Lake Albert. With this objective in mind we paid a visit to SOTEXCO, a cotton trading company, which we understood had vehicles using the river road. The director was as helpful as he could be.

'We have a truck leaving this morning for a plantation 100 km [62 miles] from here, but that's as far as we go. You'll have to walk the 80 km [50 miles] from there to Panga. The road from Panga to Bomili is too bad for lorries, so you would have to walk another 80 km [50 miles] there.' It was a toss-up as to whether we took this option immediately or looked into other possibilities first. We decided to pursue other options. As things were to develop, we should have taken the bird in the hand. We moved on to the *Commissaire de Zone*, the local administrative officer, who was less than encouraging about our chances of progressing further.

'It will take you nine days by *pirogue* to Panga, if you can find anyone willing to take you. There's only one man in Banalia who owns an outboard motor and he's at Panga now. I don't know when he will be back, maybe tomorrow, maybe next week. As for the road, there's a bridge down so it's impossible to get a truck right through to Panga.'

Whilst there, we broached the subject of Major Barttelot. We were keen to trace his grave, or failing that, perhaps there were still old men in the town who might remember stories of the white man murdered near here 100 years ago. The *Commissaire* had not the faintest idea what we were talking about, or why we should be interested in such a thing, but was polite enough to suggest that he would have someone look into the matter.

That evening, over a few drinks with a passing truck driver, it was suggested that we could hire bicycles or, failing that, the *Commissaire's* Landcruiser. At the time these sounded like good ideas, but they soon evaporated in the cold light of morning. There was the insurmountable problem of returning bicycles to Banalia. As to the Landcruiser, we were told by the *Commissaire*, after a little hesitation, that it was 'in Kisangani'. There was still no sign of the outboard canoe nor any news of its impending return. However, there was news of an elderly man with a story of a white man's grave a few miles down river from the town. The body, said to be one of Stanley's men, had been exhumed and returned to Europe some years ago and now only a few traces remained. It was worth pursuing, so we arranged to come back later and meet the man. Our next port of call, on what was to become a regular morning round, was the offices of the cotton company. We now regretted having rejected the lift on their lorry the previous day as it was obvious that theirs was the only transport on the road. We enquired when the next one would run.

'Sorry, we have no trucks scheduled to go for at least a week, maybe longer. There's a possibility that we might have one going 50 km tomorrow to repair the road, but that's not definite.' There didn't seem to be much point in getting stranded 50 km [31 miles] down the road. If we couldn't find transport in Banalia, we certainly wouldn't find any there. Passing the time in a bar, we learnt what could be the real reason for our difficulties. Panga, we discovered, had certain special attractions. It was a centre for illegal goldpanning. The road route was permanently blocked to discourage visitors and the outboard-powered canoe on which we had been pinning our hopes was used to bring in supplies to the miners. The owner, no doubt, made huge profits on this trade and was unlikely to welcome passengers. Even if he did, the price he would charge would be exorbitant. Our chances of following the river were fading fast.

Later, we were introduced to a *Chef de Collectivité*, the headman of a group of villages outside Banalia, and the source of the white man's grave story. He was a great ball of a man, weighing about 20 stone, probably around 60 years old and prosperous-looking in a new green flowery shirt. He promised to take us to the spot the next day as an act of 'friendship to our foreign visitors'. We gratefully accepted his offer.

Early next morning we were collected from the hotel and set off paddling downstream in a *pirogue* to pick up the Chief. Shortly after setting out, a piece of paper was passed back to us. This turned out to be an itemised bill for the day's trip, totalling 4500 zaïres, the equivalent of £60. So much for 'international friendship'. The Chief came aboard and the canoe rolled ominously as he settled his bulk in the stern. His wife handed him a large bundle containing his lunch and we were on our way. The river flowed away in a sweeping arc, the banks

The empty grave down river from Banalia that was not Major Barttelot's last resting place.

densely forested and the water's edge covered in deep beds of purple-flowering water hyacinth.

After an hour's paddling, when we had gone about three or four miles, the dugout nosed into a mass of tangled tree roots by the bank and we were there. We scrambled through the thick undergrowth to find, about 20 yards from the water's edge, a large hole in the ground about 6 feet long, 3 feet wide and 4 feet deep. This was the grave. We stood around examining the area. It seemed faintly ridiculous to travel so far in order to stare into a nondescript hole in the ground. Two of the men with us, no doubt sensing our disappointment, volunteered the information that they had been in the party that had exhumed the body. They were rather vague about dates but it seemed to have been just before the Second World War. Warming to the subject, another man added that he was the grandson of the local chief who had given permission for the white man to be buried at this spot, known as Babuli, near the village of Loseke. The man was apparently killed in fighting with Arab slave traders up river at Panga. The only name he was known by was *Mbalabo*, saviour, in this case saviour of the local villagers from the Arab slavers. By the time that the body reached Banalia, it was in such a state of decomposition that it was decided to bury it there and then. When it was later exhumed, there was found to be a skeleton but no head, seeming to confirm the Arab connection. The Arabs were in the habit of lopping off and removing heads as evidence of their success. One thing was certain, this hole had not been the last resting place of Major Barttelot. Our informant had not quite finished his story. The most important part was the present he received for helping to recover the body, a 12-bore shotgun and a box of cartridges. Africans have a very long memory for presents, and no doubt he was hopeful that we would be equally grateful.

Having exhausted the possibilities of the hole in the ground, we boarded the canoe for the return journey. It was agony. We did not have the luxury of the chairs so thoughtfully provided for us on our earlier trip with Victor. Here we had to squat in an awkward cramped position on a strip of bamboo, with our knees braced against the sides of the canoe. We were soon stiff and sore as the paddlers made their slow and laborious way against the current. After a couple of hours of this torment, the Chief's village came into sight and we were soon more comfortably ensconced on his verandah enjoying a beer and handing over the extortionate fee. Parting from our money was made easier by virtue of the fact that he was a jolly rogue who made no bones about robbing us. He was an educated man who had worked for the colonial administration from 1945 and had visited Europe several times. He had now retired to his home village as a respected elder statesman to share his twilight years with a nubile young wife one-third his age. We wished him luck, refused the offer of the canoe to cover the two miles back to Banalia, and set off to stretch our aching limbs with a walk. Like small towns everywhere, it is impossible to keep one's business private. As we walked along, numerous enquiries were made as to whether we had found 'the white man's grave'. The people must have thought us very odd, paying large sums to view an empty grave, particularly when the late occupant wasn't even a relative.

It was becoming clear that we might spend weeks patrolling Banalia without finding transport. The Aruwimi had thwarted us again. Reluctantly, we decided on the one option we had so far avoided considering. We would return to Kisangani and take the main road northeast to Bunia, close to Lake Albert. We consoled ourselves with the thought that we would still be following Stanley's general route, and would cross his path at least twice, first at Avakubi, in Stanley's time the Arab camp of Ugarrowwa's, and again at Fort Bodo, the expedition advance camp not far from the town of Mambasa.

Every day since we had arrived, there had been trucks and pick-ups crossing the ferry from the north bank of the river and heading south for Kisangani. But now that we had decided to go that way, the flow of traffic completely dried up. All we could find was a minibus whose driver told us that he would be going to Kisangani the following day, provided he could get a full load of passengers together.

Irebu Monganga, Chef de Collectivité, *centre with baby daughter, poses before his house after the sortie to the empty grave site.*

'I'll reserve two seats for you,' he promised.

We were up early next morning and were soon packed up and positioned on the hotel verandah to await developments. No south-bound truck passed, but at 11 am, just as it started to rain, the minibus drew up outside and the driver waved cheerily. It was a 16-seater and already had 30 passengers. Our rucksacks went on the roof rack along with assorted bundles, two bikes, several hens in baskets, two pigs and a goat, all very much alive. We clambered aboard and squeezed on to the double seat which, amazingly, had been reserved for us. To be more accurate, two-thirds of the seat was ours; the rest was already occupied by a woman and her baby. The bus wheezed off down the road to Kisangani.

Progress was slow. There were toilet stops, lunch stops, several stops to clear the carburettor, and a more lengthy stop when we ran out of petrol. The driver set off on foot with a can in search of fuel at a mission a few miles away. It had been raining off and on and we took the opportunity to try to get our rucksacks under cover. They looked very soggy and we hoped that this was due to the rain rather than to the pigs and goat who squealed and kicked overhead whenever we hit a bump in the road. Eventually the driver returned and we drove on to the mission to fill up. The amount that went into the tank looked suspiciously small and, sure enough, seven miles out of Kisangani the bus ground to a halt once again. By now it was 8.30 pm and very dark. One of the bikes on the roof was lifted down and its owner dispatched to Kisangani with three jerrycans strapped to his machine. The rest of us settled down for the night as best we could. As dawn spread into day,

Lieutenant Stairs is wounded by a poisoned arrow on the march through the Ituri Forest.

we were still stranded by the roadside. Our numbers had decreased slightly as one or two hardy souls had set off to complete their journey on foot. There was still no sign of the petrol, so the second bicycle was taken down and another emissary set off into the distance. At 8.30 am, with no change in our situation, we were delighted when the lorry of a trader we had met in Banalia appeared on the scene. We jumped at the chance of a lift. The lorry had been chartered by two market mamas who had filled it with fruit and vegetables for sale in Kisangani market. They had left Banalia at 2 am, taking six and a half hours to cover the same distance on which we had spent 21½ hours! Some miles on we passed the first cyclist returning with just one can of petrol. We hoped it was enough to allow the others to complete their journey.

At the bridge over the River Tshopo, the lorry was stopped by police who demanded 1000 zaïres from the driver, but

finally let him pass on the payment of 150 zaïres. The driver shrugged. This was a way of life in Zaïre. Entering the town, the lorry stopped at a market to unload the produce. Once more the police appeared on the scene and, on the excuse of some irregularity with the truck, demanded 500 zaïres. After a long-drawn-out dispute, the matter was settled and the driver dropped us at the door of the Hotel Olympia, exactly a week since we had left it and 24 hours after leaving Banalia.

*****

Stanley pressed steadily on through the forest. He met some opposition from the natives, but his superior fire power kept them at bay. The first desertions happened 23 days into the march on 20 July 1887. This was unusually good going, but the situation was soon to deteriorate. On 2 July the first death occurred in camp, and the poor and irregular diet started to take its toll. The 14th saw the expedition

81

attacked by a new and deadly weapon, the poisoned arrow. Ten men, including Lieutenant Stairs, were hit. The Lieutenant was the only survivor, the others dying horribly and slowly of lockjaw over the next few days. By 22 July there were 16 men dead or missing, and 57 too sick to walk. Tropical ulcers presented the main problem. A simple scratch could turn into a putrid wound in a matter of days, eating through the flesh to expose the bone. Parke, the doctor, added the gruesome detail that as the unfortunate men slept at night, rats would come and feast on the vile pulsating sores. The doctor knew better than anyone the suffering endured by the men and commented:

'It is marvellous how our men obey us so well, stick to their loads under such extreme hardships.'

Things were to get much worse. The 30 August, by Stanley's calculations, saw the expedition at the half-way mark. This bit of good news was passed on to the men but was met only by 'murmurs of disbelief'. The month closed with the worst of all discoveries: the Arabs were already established on the river. At first the canoe flying the red flag which they met coming down river was thought to belong to Emin, but they soon learnt that it bore the flag of Zanzibar and the men in it were scouts for the ivory and slave trader Uledi Balyuz, also known as Ugarrowwa. The scouts reported that their headquarters were eight days' march further up river and that their own camp was just one day away. Stanley knew only too well the consequences of this news: the countryside would be laid waste, food would be even more difficult to find and the loyalty of his own men would be tested.

It was no surprise when over the next few days 12 porters absconded with their loads. He would have to act to put a stop to the disintegration of the expedition. On 4 September a man was caught red-handed in the act of deserting. Stanley wanted to make an example of him, but the headmen persuaded him against execution. Instead, all the men were mustered, 60 of the least reliable identified, and the rifles of these men made useless on the premise that to venture alone in the forest unarmed was suicide. This slowed the loss of men and goods, but did not entirely quench the trickling away of the life blood of the expedition. The column struggled on, food a perennial problem. Foraging parties now returned with berries, fungi and forest rats which they had previously ignored. Seventeen days after their first contact with Arabs, the expedition arrived at Ugarrowwa's headquarters and made camp on the opposite bank. As was usual in these encounters, the Arabs were courteous and generous in their hospitality.

The chief, Uledi Balyuz, had first travelled to Central Africa as a tent-boy with the Speke and Grant expedition in the early 1860s, had deserted and had eventually set up as a successful trader. Unfortunately for Stanley, he was a shining example to the Zanzibari porters of what an expedition deserter could achieve. Uledi seems to have been keen to be of service to Stanley. Firstly, he made a speech to the porters stating that any deserters who came to his camp would be put in irons and returned to their master; secondly, he agreed to carry a message down river to the Rear Column; and thirdly, offered food and accommodation for the expedition's sick until they could be recalled by Stanley. In return he would receive three hundred-weight of powder, to be collected from the Rear Column, and trade goods in payment for the upkeep of the sick.

The expedition had been on the road for 82 days and had covered about 370 miles. The cost had been 62 men either dead or deserted, and 56 men too ill to walk. The sick were left with the Arabs. Thirty per cent of the manpower of the expedition had been lost. Every day in the ravaged and inhospitable terrain, food had to be found to feed some 270 hungry men, who were entirely dependent on whatever they could scavenge en route. For many days there would be nothing at all, then suddenly they would find a plantation and there would be plenty. Stanley constantly bemoaned the fact that the men seemed incapable of conserving their supplies. The Europeans were not immune to similar problems. Hoffman, Stanley's servant, recorded the situation: 'Even the white men, although they knew better how to reserve their small supply of food, began to quarrel among themselves. The darkness, the downpour of rain . . . the interminable peals of thunder . . . all combined to make us nervous and irritable, so that often we would not speak to each other for days on end.' On 30 September the followers of another Arab, Kilonga-Longa, appeared in camp. Stanley had already heard that this man was active higher up river. The new arrivals advised him that their station was five days' march further on, and ominously, that no food was to be had before that point.

After six days' march, there was no sign of the Arab camp, food was non-existent and the column was in terrible shape. Since leaving the last Arab settlement with 271 fit men, eight had died or deserted and 52 were too weak and sick to go on, including Captain Nelson. Survival was the only question now. With customary ruthlessness, Stanley made his decision. The sick were left behind to fend for themselves whilst the main body pressed on to find relief. For 11 more days they struggled on until at last coming to Kilonga-Longa's village and salvation.

The date was 17 October 1887, 112 days and 475 miles from Yambuya. The promise to return for the Rear Column by November was forgotten. The Arabs at the village were the advance guard for their chief, Kilonga-Longa, who was still to arrive this far north. Perhaps because of the chief's absence, Stanley's treatment at the hands of these Arabs did not take its usual generous form. Food had to be paid for and they were not prepared to take IOUs. The porters started selling the only things of value to which they had

access, the rifles and ammunition. Within a couple of days 11 rifles and 3000 rounds of ammunition were missing, and another poor wretch was hanged for the crime. Eventually there was a confrontation with the Arabs and some improvement in the situation followed, but it was eight days before they could get together a relief party to go to the rescue of Captain Nelson and the men left on the trail. On 26 October, Mounteney Jephson led a party back down river. The plan was to bring the survivors to the Arab camp where they would stay, tended by Surgeon Parke, whilst Jephson and any fit men would follow Stanley's trail. A further 29 men from the main group, too sick to continue, were also left in camp. Stanley marched away at the head of a column now reduced to just 146 men.

After 12 days, they came to the limit of the area of Arab influence and, like a dream, the world changed. There were villages, plantations, even livestock. A halt was called at a place named Ibwiri to allow Jephson to catch up with the party. In the meantime, everyone took advantage of the abundance of food in the area to build up their wasted bodies.

Jephson arrived in camp on 16 November 1887, having successfully carried out his mission to bring Captain Nelson from his forest camp to the Arab village of Kilonga-Longa, but that was the full extent of the good news. Of the 52 men who had stayed behind with Nelson, only five were left. The rest had died, deserted or were wandering in the depths of the forest searching for food. The situation at the Arab village was little better. The officers were reduced to bartering their clothes for food, the men, with nothing to sell, were in a much worse position. Their relief would have to wait. The first priority was to push on as quickly as possible to the lake and make contact with Emin Pasha. The column now numbered 175 souls. Over 200 men had paid with their lives or their health to advance the enterprise some 550 miles, and they were still in the forest.

As the expedition moved further east, the nature of the terrain changed. The forest became more open and easier to traverse, and hills were more frequent. The villages they passed through were large and prosperous, but still the people would have nothing to do with the expedition, simply fading away into the forest at its approach. On 2 December they entered a village where the huts were thatched with grass, a material unknown in the forest. The great day came on 4 December. They crossed a river, forced their way through a thicket on the far bank and there before them was open grassland. Stanley recorded the moment:

. . . then, to our undisguised joy, [we] emerged upon a rolling plain, green as an English lawn, into broadest, sweetest daylight, and warm and glorious sunshine, to inhale the pure air with an uncontrollable rapture. . . . We strode forward at a pace most unusual, and finally, unable to suppress our emotions, the whole caravan broke into a run.

They had struggled and suffered for 160 days, covering 620 miles, in the dim depths of a forest without a blade of grass or the open sky to be seen. But they had not yet reached their goal, and early on found indications that the local people would not let Stanley have his own way without a fight. In village huts they found well-crafted weapons, shields and body armour capable of stopping pistol shots. It seemed that these people would be very different adversaries from the ill-equipped forest natives.

In the following days the natives assembled in their thousands, lining ridges and high points along the expedition's line of march. Skirmishes and even set-piece battles took place but, in spite of the natives' bravery, Stanley's superior fire power kept them at bay. For nine

The officers and men are overjoyed as they finally break free of the forest.

days they marched and fought their way across the grassy plain until, breasting a hill, the plateau dropped sheer away in front of them. Far below was a barren plain and in the hazy distance the Albert Nyanza. They had finally made it.

Once down at the lake shore, realisation began to dawn that the end of the journey was an anticlimax. All their efforts had been concentrated on the single objective of arriving at Lake Albert. But now arrival was not enough. There was no grateful Pasha waiting to greet them with open arms, just an inhospitable empty plain and a depressing expanse of open water. As Stanley wrote in his diary, 'It would be too hard if our long travels were to be quite in vain.' After two days' aimless wandering along the lake shore, all they had learnt was that no white man had visited this south-western corner of the lake for years. No message was waiting for them. Travel on the lake was impossible.

The first sight of Lake Albert.

They had left their boat far back in the forest, and locally there were only a few small two-man canoes unsuitable for long distances on choppy water. They could not even build a boat, as the grasslands did not boast a single tree big enough to make a canoe. As usual, Stanley was under pressure. The men must be fed, back in the forest more men and officers were awaiting relief from their leader, and there were worries about the amount of ammunition that remained. It is worth remembering that the object of the expedition was to deliver sufficient supplies of ammunition to Emin Pasha to allow him to make an independent decision on his future course of action. It would be highly embarrassing for Stanley if, on meeting Emin, he had to admit that all the ammunition had been used up on the way. Another fact that had to be taken into account was that Stanley had been out of contact with the world for more

85

than eight months. For all he knew, Emin might already have left and even now be safely on the East Coast. All things considered, Stanley felt that his only option was to retreat, re-group and try again later. On 16 December 1887, the expedition turned its back on the waters of Lake Albert and marched into the forest.

The retreat was to the village of Ibwiri, about 120 miles from the lake, where an abundance of food had been found on their first visit. Here the expedition arrived on 6 January 1888 and immediately set to work to build a strong stockade. This was completed by 18 January and re-named Fort Bodo. With a secure base to work from, Stanley set about resolving other outstanding questions. On reflection, he had already concluded that his failure to find Emin at the lake was the Pasha's fault: 'now that the Governor . . . had either departed homeward, or could, or would not assist in his own relief, the various matters thrust aside for his sake required immediate attention.' Lieutenant Stairs was dispatched to Kilonga-Longa's to escort the sick and the two officers, Nelson and Parke, back to Fort Bodo, and to retrieve the boat. This task was completed by 12 February. Four days later, the tireless Stairs was on the march again, this time all the way to Ugarrowwa's to bring back the men left there. The Rear Column was also remembered. Stanley prepared dispatches for Major Barttelot which were taken by Stairs to the Arab camp for forwarding. Stairs' instructions were to be back at Fort Bodo by 25 March, the date on which Stanley planned to leave for another attempt to find Emin at the lake. Whilst he was away, the rest of the expedition set about making themselves secure and comfortable at the fort.

Although the men's condition showed marked improvement, Stanley had been struck down with a recurring gastric complaint and was to be confined to bed for over three weeks. A further complication was his badly infected arm, a condition aggravated by an incident recorded by Jephson: 'two days ago it was nearly well but in one of his ungovernable fits of rage—which by the way are of very frequent occurrence—he hit his German servant across the head with a stick and it has made his arm really bad.' In the latter part of March he started to improve, and by the end of the month felt ready to start the task again. Stairs had still not reappeared, but he decided that they could wait no longer. Leaving Fort Bodo in the charge of Captain Nelson and a small garrison, Stanley, Jephson and Parke led 126 men back to the lake. This time they had their boat with them, so were better equipped to find the Pasha or, as Stanley put it, 'penetrate the silence around him'.

When the expedition reached the grasslands again, their reception by the natives was quite different from their first visit. There was no fighting; regular supplies of food were delivered to the column and men were provided to carry loads. It was almost as though Stanley, the conquering hero, was returning home. It is always a wonder to the traveller in Africa how quickly news can travel. By simple word of mouth, whole regions know what is happening quicker than if each had received a telegram. Already Stanley's first appearance had been reported far to the north of Lake Albert and on up the Nile. There it had also come to the ears of one Emin Pasha.

On reaching the edge of the plateau, Stanley was handed a package wrapped in oil-cloth by the local chief, Kavalli. It contained a letter from the Governor of Equatoria Province, Emin Pasha, asking Stanley to send word of his arrival, upon which he, Emin, would come to meet him. The letter, dated 25 March, was received on 18 April. Two days later the expedition boat, the *Advance*, was taken to the lake and Jephson dispatched to carry Stanley's response. Stanley wrote explaining his mission and confirming that he would await Emin's arrival. He took the opportunity to suggest that the Pasha should not come empty-handed: 15,000

lb of grain and three or four milk cows would be useful. The nearest of Emin's stations was only a few days north on Lake Albert, but Stanley was comfortable enough where he was. He set up camp at the village of Bundi and prepared to wait.

On 29 April a note came from Jephson saying that messengers had been dispatched to the Pasha. The camp moved to the lake shore to be closer to hand. That same day a steamer was spotted at around 4.30 pm. The boat slowly approached and dropped anchor some way off shore at about 6.30 pm. Initially, the exuberant firing of guns by the Zanzibari porters was misinterpreted and shots were returned, but matters were soon sorted out and Emin came ashore. It was now quite dark. The historic meeting took place outside Stanley's tent. Three men approached: Jephson, Casati (an Italian traveller) and Emin.

All shook hands and then Stanley had to ask which was Emin Pasha. 'Then one rather small, slight figure, wearing glasses, arrested my attention by saying in excellent English, "I owe you a thousand thanks, Mr Stanley".' In spite of all the deprivations of the march, Stanley had managed to preserve some bottles of champagne for the occasion. They were the only luxury he could provide. Emin, on the other hand, appeared to have an abundance of everything. The comparisons must have been painful: poor Stanley, the rescuer, in patched clothing, his followers in rags, Emin, object of the relief mission, in a newly pressed white suit, his men smartly uniformed, even accompanied by a band!

The next day a ceremony took place in which Stanley handed over the sum total of his relief of Equatoria province: 31

cases of Remington ammunition, enough for a couple of brief skirmishes, and a suit of clothing for Emin, which was far too big. The preliminaries over, the two men got down to discussing what action Emin intended taking. This was not going to be an easy question to answer. The two men were to spend 24 days together, at the end of which Stanley claimed to have no more idea of Emin's intentions than on their first day of meeting. Stanley, the man of action and command, had met in Emin the sort of man he simply could not abide, a ditherer.

At the time of this first meeting, Emin Pasha was 48 years old. Stanley's servant, Hoffman, described him as 'a short, slight man with a brisk, businesslike manner, a close-cropped beard, and small myopic eyes hidden behind thick glasses.' As to his background, this was something that was difficult to establish accurately as Emin went to some trouble to obscure his origins and early activity for personal reasons. The basic facts seem to be that he was born Eduard Karl Oskar Theodor Schnitzer on 28 March 1840 in the town of Oppeln in Prussian Silesia, of Jewish parentage. After leaving school, he studied medicine at the Universities of Breslau, Königsberg and Berlin, where he qualified in 1864. After submitting his application too late, he was not allowed to sit the examination which would have qualified him to practise medicine in Germany, a state of affairs which forced him to look abroad. Late in 1864 he arrived in the port of Antivari, then part of the Turkish Empire, where he was to stay for the next seven years, eventually rising to the position of district and port medical officer. He next joined the staff of a Turkish official named Ismail Hakki Pasha, a kind of roving ambassador, with whom he travelled extensively through the Middle East over the next few years. It was at this time that he adopted his first alias, *M le docteur Hairoullah Effendi*, and appears to have formed a relationship with Ismail's wife, a Rumanian woman of his own age. Following Ismail's death, Emin arrived unannounced at the Prussian family home in Neisse with Madame Ismail, four children and a party of slave girls, an event that must have been something of a shock for his family and for the conservative mores of small town Germany in 1875. Emin presented Madame Ismail as his wife, although it is unlikely that they were in fact married. He soon tired of these heavy responsibilities and simply disappeared.

He next surfaced, penniless, in Khartoum in December 1875. His abilities as a conversationalist in many languages, a chess player and an accomplished pianist found him a place in the small European community. He was looked after by an Austrian called Giegeler and the German Consul, Rosset. Eventually, in April 1876, Giegeler managed to secure a position for Emin with General Gordon, then governor of Equatoria province. It was at about this time that the name Emin was adopted. The truth of its origins is not clear, but it may be considered something more than pure coincidence that the previous medical officer who had served under Gordon and who had been shipped home sick, passing through Khartoum early in 1876, was named Emin Effendi. So Schnitzer, the new Emin, joined Gordon and started his long association with Equatoria. Within a few months Gordon left the province to take on other tasks, whilst Emin served under a number of governors who came and went in quick succession until, in July 1878, he in turn became governor.

Emin ran his province quietly and efficiently, his only contact with the Egyptian government being the occasional steamer from Khartoum. He was largely left to his own devices, a situation which suited him very well. The post of governor allowed him plenty of spare time to pursue his love of natural history. He was well known to the museums and learned societies of Europe, regularly keeping in contact and sending specimens for their collections.

Equatoria was the remotest province of the Sudan, a string of stations extending from the northern end of Lake Albert along the Nile. It was in fact the 'Siberia' of the Sudan, a penal colony where the criminals and malcontents of the Egyptian army and government were sent to serve out their days. The governor could not discipline or dismiss his subordinates, his authority extending no further than the right to move officials from one station to another. The province was run on the basis of a mutual agreement to pursue a quiet and relatively comfortable life, a convenient arrangement that started to crumble with the rise of the Mahdist Movement in 1881. In 1883 the steamers stopped arriving from Khartoum and Equatoria was cut off from the outside world.

General Gordon was recalled to the Sudan in 1884 to save the day. In January 1885 Khartoum fell and Gordon perished with it. Shortly afterwards, the Sudan was to all intents and purposes abandoned to its fate. Late in 1884, Equatoria came under attack, much to Emin's surprise, and in spite of the laxity of the officers, the native troops fought well and checked the advance of the Mahdi's forces. Emin fell back to defend his southern stations. His northern division ignored his order and decided to stay put. From that point on Emin had no authority at all over one half of his forces, and only a tenuous hold over the other half. The initial opposition encountered by the Mahdi's General, Keremallah, caused him to pause and await reinforcements. The immediate threat to Equatoria was lifted.

As the troubles in the area were building up, two travellers who had been exploring independently in the region found their way to Emin's headquarters to seek sanctuary. These were the Russian explorer Dr Junker and the Italian traveller Captain Casati. Junker managed to break out of Equatoria in 1886 and eventually made his way to the East Coast. Through his efforts, some letters and supplies got through to Emin, whilst Emin's calls for assistance were broadcast to the world via the missionaries stationed by Lake Victoria. His epistles were to prompt the public interest which would lead to the raising of the Emin Pasha Relief Expedition. One of the letters that Emin received was from the Egyptian Prime Minister, Nubar Pasha, coolly advising him that the Sudan had been abandoned and that he was free to stay or leave as he felt fit. He was now truly cut off. In a letter Emin commented bitterly: 'It seems tolerably certain that our difficulties have not been realised either in Egypt or elsewhere; people simply point out the way to Zanzibar, as if the matter were a promenade to Shabra.' Emin had in mind that any withdrawal would include all his forces and their dependents, some 8000–10,000 people. It was obviously an impossible task to march them to the coast. However, Emin's estimate of the loyalty of his followers was extravagantly optimistic, and would remain so to the end.

When Stanley eventually mounted the Equatoria stage, Emin was only a bit player in its affairs. Although still governor in name, the reality was that control had been wrested from him and the province was now run by a group of dissident officers. With no immediate threat from the Mahdi to the north the officers were unlikely to want to exchange their comfortable existence for a return to Egypt and the government that had banished them to Equatoria in the first place. It is perhaps not surprising that on the shores of Lake Albert, Emin, the governor without power, and Stanley, the saviour short of the means of salvation, had difficulty in agreeing a course of action. Hoffman was again on hand to record Stanley's attitude: 'the Englishman could not understand or condone Emin's continual attitude of "wait and see". It seemed absurd to him that we should have come all this way, and endured so much, only to be politely told that there was nothing wrong.'

Stanley offered various options and

attempted to establish the Pasha's attitude to each. He had handed over dispatches from the Egyptian government confirming their earlier instructions to Emin that Equatoria was abandoned and that he was a free agent to stay or leave as he saw fit. The sting in the tail was that back pay would be given only to those who returned to Cairo. Those who decided to stay would forfeit all right to their salaries. The Egyptian government was continually short of money and more than happy to save the estimated minimum of £50,000 owed to the men serving in Equatoria. Emin Pasha dismissed this question of pay, and, as recorded by Stanley, made one of the few clear statements he was to make about anything:

There can be only about two thousand and odd pounds due. What is such a sum to a man about to be shelved? I am now forty eight and one of my eyes is utterly gone. When I get to Egypt they will give me some fine words and bow me out. And all I have to do is to seek out some corner of Cairo or Stamboul for a final resting-place. A fine prospect truly!

Even if he himself rejected the government's offer, Emin thought, or hoped, that his Egyptian officers and clerks would want to return. They had been a constant source of trouble to him and he would be pleased to see the last of them.

Two days later, Stanley judged that the moment was right to broach the subject of the offers that his patrons, King Leopold and Sir William Mackinnon, had authorised him to make. Leopold's proposal was to incorporate Equatoria into the Congo Free State. Emin would receive a handsome salary and in return would be required not only to run the province at a profit, but also to open up and maintain a line of communication back to the Congo River. This would entail the conversion of the route travelled at such cost by Stanley to a regular road, at that time a seemingly impossible task. The viability of Equatoria depended on good lines of communication. The Nile would be the only realistic route for many years to come. Leopold's terms could not be met. The offer from Mackinnon was altogether more vague. It involved Emin's abandoning Equatoria and moving all his people to an area to the north-east of Lake Victoria. There he was to establish himself and maintain a toe-hold on the lake until such time as a line of communication could be pushed through from the newly gained East Coast concession. He and his people would then be a part of the Imperial British East Africa Company's assets. Emin's response to the Egyptian instruction had been that he could not walk away from Equatoria and abandon those of his loyal followers who chose to stay. Mackinnon's alternative seemed to offer a workable compromise. This was the course of action that Emin favoured, but he would not make a decision alone. He would do whatever his people wanted.

*****

Stanley had succeeded in his initial objective of reaching Lake Albert, but we were still far from emulating his achievement. On our return to Kisangani, after the abortive trip to Banalia, we had hoped to find some eastbound transport amongst the regular procession of overlanders who passed though the Hotel Olympia. Needless to say, the place was deserted, the only resident being a young Japanese traveller camping in the grounds. From what we could gather, he spoke no language other than his own. He was touring Africa on a bicycle so there was not much chance of a lift there.

In the bar we fell into conversation with Eugene, half-Zaïrean, half-Kenyan, one of those young men one finds all over the world who seem to be able to earn a living by making themselves useful to passing tourists. He was bemoaning the absence of the overland trucks that were his main source of business, but bucked up when he heard that we were looking for transport. He would fix it for us, no trouble. Whilst Eugene was beavering away on our behalf, we took advantage of our second enforced stay in Kisangani to pursue our Stanley researches. We had heard that the Catholic Archbishop Fataki was something of an expert on the history of Zaïre, so we set off to try to arrange an interview with him. The great rambling church and *Procure*, the central supply depot for the outlying missions, stood on high ground near the port, overlooking the river. The *Procure* was a huge fortress-like building with one entrance which could be barred in times of siege— and no doubt had been during past troubles—by a pair of stout wooden gates. Security was a prime consideration as the stores here held more goods and equipment than could be found in any one place in the rest of the region. The Catholics were well organised to be independent of the fickle supply system to which most of Zaïre was subject.

With surprising ease we were ushered into the presence of the Archbishop. There was a moment's embarrassment as we were not quite sure of the protocol required for such an occasion. Should we kiss his ring, fall to the ground on bended knee, or simply shake hands? His charming smile and calm serenity dispelled any worries about formality as, with a sweep of his arm, he guided us to a group of easy chairs. Monseigneur Fataki was a small, sprightly, round-faced man in his eighties who listened to our story with quiet attention. The two books he had written were on the founding of the town of Kisangani and the establishment of the Catholic church in the area. He explained that he was no expert on the Emin Pasha Expedition. He could not throw any light on the whereabouts of Barttelot's grave, but was a little more encouraging on the prospects of finding some evidence of Stanley's passing.

'Now, there are two things that I know of: Fort Bodo is a marked site that you will find 26 km [16 miles] beyond Mambasa on the road to Lake Albert, and the other thing is an inscribed stone marking the place where Stanley had his camp above the lake. At least, they both used to be marked. It is many years since I have been that way.'

We mentioned that we had been surprised by the absence in the villages of any oral tradition connected with Stanley. After all, the events which we were talking about had occurred in quite recent history.

'That should not be a surprise,' he suggested. 'During colonial times many villagers, and particularly the traditional chiefs, were, as a matter of policy, dispersed to other areas. And, of course, their history went with them. The people who may well have preserved their oral traditions are the pygmies. Why don't you go and see Father Carlo at Mambasa. He, I believe, is something of an authority on these people. I'm sure he could help you.'

We would indeed go to see Father Carlo, if we could ever find any transport to get there. Our fixer, Eugene, had so far drawn a blank, and we opened another line of investigation through Dimitri, the hotel proprietor, who would put the word around the Greek community, many of whom were in the transport business. We, in turn, did the rounds of likely companies. It was clear that travel in Zaïre was becoming increasingly difficult. There is no public transport to speak of and in order to get about, most people rely on finding a place on the back of a lorry. There were now fewer and fewer lorries where this was possible. As companies bought new vehicles, they were choosing container carriers and trucks with closed backs. This made obvious sense from a security point of view, but severely restricted the amount of passenger space available, as it was possible to travel only in the cab. Our difficulty in getting out of Kisangani was not that there was no transport on the road, but rather that no one had passenger space.

There seemed to be more hopeful news on the travel front when we met Eugene the next day.

'There might be a chance,' he said rather

doubtfully. 'There's an Indian truck driver leaving for Bunia sometime tomorrow afternoon. He may take you, but John and I had better go and have a talk with him tomorrow morning.'

I hoped that I would be included on the passenger list, even if not considered worthy to take part in the negotiations. After the meeting John reported back.

'He doesn't seem too friendly. He ignored me completely and would only speak to Eugene. According to him the driver said he would be leaving about 6 pm, but his men told us that it was more likely to be 3 pm. He doesn't seem keen to take us.'

It didn't look too promising, but as we had no other options in sight, we decided we might as well go along and try our luck. We packed up, said goodbye to the chimps, the cats and the parrot, who had almost, but not quite, mastered 'Colonel Bogey', and set off up the road with our bags trundling along behind us in what must have been the squeakiest of all the handcarts for hire in Kisangani.

It was a good thing that we did arrive early as the driver left at 4 pm. He had a huge 40-ton Mercedes truck with a 10-ton trailer and was, according to Eugene, only 19 years old, so we hoped that he could handle this monster. He still did not appear to be on speaking terms with us, but passed a message through Eugene (who had earlier suggested that the ride would be free) that we should pay him 2500 zaïres for the journey to Mambasa. I thought this was a bit steep as it didn't include seats in the cab. Instead we climbed 10 feet up the side of the truck on a metal ladder and then hauled ourselves over the edge into a small space, free of cargo (the cargo, incidentally, was a mammoth consignment of flour and Coca-Cola), but occupied by various lumpy sacks and a spare wheel. The other human occupants of this space were two young female passengers and three men who worked for the driver, loading, unloading, changing tyres and brewing up tea and coffee on a paraffin stove whenever required. They all seemed to have taken their cue from the driver and were unfriendly and surly. This was not the sort of reception we were used to in Zaïre. The driver's name, we learnt, was Fouad Hassan. Although Eugene had described him as an Indian, his name and appearance suggested he was Lebanese or even Arab. Perhaps he was the link we had been looking for with the Emin Pasha Relief Expedition, a descendant of one of the Arab slave raiders whom Stanley had encountered on his march through the forest, or even perhaps of Tippu Tip himself! But even if Fouad Hassan knew the history of his ancestry, he did not look as though he would reveal it to us. Completing the cast of characters were two who were honoured with seats in the cab: the relief driver and a large fearsome lady who insisted on addressing me throughout the journey as 'mondeli', white. I'm sure if I had responded by calling her 'black,' I would have been accused of racism.

Even if the company was not of our choice, we were at least on the move again. The huge lorry roared through the gears and started to eat up the battered tarmac road towards the jungle. The town was soon left behind, the road became a thin red laterite line and the tall trees closed in all around. We made good progress, covering over 186 miles, and continued until just before midnight when the driver stopped in a small village where there were rooms for travellers. As it was rumoured that we would be leaving again at 6 am, we assumed, as we didn't yet trust Fouad and didn't want to be left behind, that this meant an earlier departure. We didn't think it worthwhile taking a room and spent an uncomfortable few hours trying to sleep in the truck. We were right about the departure time. At 4 am there was quite a commotion when our two female travelling companions learnt that we were about to leave. They had gone to the expense of taking a room and loudly expressed their indignation at not getting value for money. After a poor

start the day continued on its downward spiral. I was soon covered from head to foot in a layer of red dust so thick that it was impossible to drag a comb through my hair.

'Think yourself lucky,' said John. 'At least it's the dry season and we're moving, not stuck in a mud hole somewhere.'

The trouble was we weren't moving, or at least not very often. At 6 am we came on a friend of Fouad's, a lorry driver with a puncture, and the next four hours were spent helping to change his wheel. 'Thank goodness,' I breathed as Fouad eventually climbed back into the cab and we got under way once more. My relief was short-lived. A quarter of an hour later we stopped again, this time for a meal break lasting one and a half hours. Another hour along the road and we had a puncture ourselves in one of the trailer wheels which entailed a further hour's delay.

We then managed to keep going for a full one and a half hours and were beginning to think we were doing well when we stopped once again, this time for an extended tea break. The theory of adapting to African standards of time when travelling was proving a little trying in practice on this journey and our lack of forward progress was the more frustrating as several lorries passed us during our frequent stops, disappearing in a cloud of red dust, never to be seen again. But at last, at 4.30 pm, we were under way once more and drove for the next four hours without a single stop.

From our vantage point high up in the lorry, we could see the forest at its best. The trees were tall and slender, often bedecked with lianas, and mixed in were dense stands of bamboo which overhung the road and cracked the unwary passenger on the head. Flowering bushes and plants could be observed down at ground level on our numerous stops. We heard birdsong then, too, normally drowned by the sound of the engine, including the laboured passage of the hornbill, a bird which sounds as though flight had been added to its abilities only as an after-

On our perch high on Fouad's lorry, we wait during one of many stops for repairs.

thought. Small villages of thatched huts lined the road, several containing the shells of brick-built villas once occupied by the colonial administrators of long-abandoned plantations. Now the roofs had caved in and tall forest trees pushed their way surrealistically through the crumbling brickwork.

At 7.30 pm it began to rain, so the men pulled the tarpaulin over our open end of the truck. I do not normally suffer from claustrophobia, but the enclosed feeling in that small, black, stuffy space very soon became almost unbearable. In this way we passed through Avakubi, the site of Ugarrowwa's settlement, crossed the bridge over the Aruwimi and arrived at Nia Nia, the village on the north bank, without even realising it! It was 8.30 pm, we had been going—or more accurately, had been on the road—for over 16 hours and had covered just 80 miles. Nia Nia was to be our night stop. It was a busy

junction where the road forked, one branch heading east to Lake Albert, the other north to the town of Isiro and beyond. Shops and food stalls along the main street were lit by the flickering light of oil lamps and all seemed to be doing good business. From a dance hall, loud pop music blared out into the dark night. Our travelling companions took rooms in the small hotel and tonight we followed suit. We did not feel much like eating, but instead discovered a life-saving drink which we were to enjoy from here on across the continent. This was a mug of *chai*, tea made with lashings of sweetened condensed milk. At home we wouldn't have touched the stuff, but here it tasted like nectar, refreshing and energy-giving. The crossing of the Aruwimi River marked our entry into the land of *chai*.

Fouad had become a little friendlier by now and actually offered to wake us next morning, as we were to make another early start. Feeling much better after a wash, but still looking rather streaky, we made ourselves as comfortable as we could in our room. It was very hot, very small, had mud walls and a compacted dirt floor, but it did have a bed with a straw-filled mattress and a sheet. We slept like logs. True to his word, Fouad knocked on the door at 4.30 am, and by 5 am we were once more on the road.

Progress was much better today. By 11 am we had reached Epulu, an attractive village of neat houses and several small hotels and restaurants. We followed Fouad and his friends into the best of the restaurants where they tucked into large plates of goat meat and rice, and we indulged our newly-acquired taste for *chai*. Epulu is visited by tourists and foreigners because of its '*Station de Capture*', a reserve where the rare okapi is bred and lives unmolested in its natural habitat. The village started life as Camp Putnam, back in 1927, when Patrick Putnam, an American anthropologist, established a camp on the banks of the Epulu River in order to do field work amongst the pygmies. His research completed, he decided to stay on and established a dispensary and leper colony. He turned his home into a guest house to help support his medical work. After his death in 1953, the name was changed to Epulu and the Belgian authorities set up the '*Station de Chasse*', now known as the '*Station de Capture*', with the aim of capturing and breeding forest animals, in particular the beautiful and vulnerable okapi.

We saw our first pygmies at Epulu. Several of the village houses had pygmy families living in the compounds, there to do the labouring jobs. Further on, we passed a pygmy camp of traditional leaf huts by the roadside. Their inhabitants were not at home, presumably hunting in the forest or gathering nuts and berries.

At 3 pm we arrived in Mambasa, again under our claustrophobic tarpaulin cover as it had come on to rain. When we emerged we found ourselves in a wide, dusty street lined with single-storey brick-built shops. We all decamped into the nearby 'Islamic Restaurant' where Fouad and friends devoured more goat stew and rice. Fouad had by now thawed out considerably and even gave us a rebate on the fare, but it was with few regrets that we said goodbye to our travelling companions.

We shouldered our heavy packs and staggered off up the hill one and a half miles to the Catholic mission. It was a large well-kept place consisting of a substantial brick church, quarters for the fathers and sisters, a dispensary, school, carpentry shop, garage and a new warehouse-type building under construction. The campsite just beyond was a welcome sight. There was a grassy area for tents and a low block containing five rooms, toilets and showers, the latter all clean and in working order. To avoid any confusion, there was also a price list posted up on the wall. It was as though a well-kept camp site in Europe had been transported to the back of beyond in Central Africa. One thing that reminded us we were still in Africa was the collection of wildlife. A monkey in a cage, a white-nosed long-tailed monkey at large, two parrots, other small cage birds, a colony of weaver birds, and two goats and their tiny kids completed the idyllic scene. We washed several pounds of red dust from ourselves and our clothes, combed our hair for the first time in three days and felt we had rejoined the human race.

The idyll was shattered when we spoke to Father Carlo, the 'expert' on pygmies. We had had enough of road transport and wanted to make the next leg of our journey east on foot through the Ituri Forest. We hoped that it would be possible to hire pygmy guides to enable us to do this. The busy priest found a few minutes to put us straight on this fantasy.

'The pygmy families round here only know their own territory. They wouldn't be able to guide you any distance through the forest. In any case numbers are small around Mambasa and we see little of them. You'll probably do better to go on to Lolwa, about 70 km [43 miles] from here. There's a big Protestant mission and a large concentration of pygmies there,' he advised us. We wondered if this was genuine advice or a case of passing the buck. He was able to confirm that the site of Fort Bodo was to be found 16 miles on the road beyond Mambasa, and added the information that 'mambasa' meant 'place of fire' and had been an overnight camp for Arab slaving parties.

Back at the Islamic Restaurant, where religious scruples didn't preclude the sale of beer, we put down our packs and began our search for transport once again. The few days at Mambasa had been a pleasant interlude, but otherwise unproductive. Two lorry drivers who stopped for refreshment were going to the town of Beni, not to Bunia near Lake Albert, and two others who were going to Bunia wouldn't take us. Finally we decided to go to Komanda, a distance of about 62 miles, where the roads to Beni, south, and Bunia, east, parted company and where, the Islamic restaurateur informed us, we would easily be able to get a lift from a pick-up taxi van. We had decided against Father Carlo's suggestion of looking for pygmies at the Lolwa mission. If our luck held true to form, there wouldn't be any pygmies there, and in any case time was getting on. We still had half the continent to cross and needed to make some forward progress.

The next ride was quite a change from our first. The other passengers, driver and crew talked and smiled a lot, even when the exhaust fell off. Makeshift repairs were carried out with cheerful efficiency and we were on our way again in 45 minutes. Fort Bodo turned out to be a low hill on which undergrowth and trees had completely obliterated any sign of the fort and the plaque marking the spot had long since disappeared. Africa seemed determined to wipe Stanley from its slate. At least this time we were not imprisoned under a tarpaulin and succeeded in seeing the non-site for ourselves.

At 5 pm we rolled into Komanda, a small settlement set around the road junction. No other traffic that evening meant a night in the roadside 'hotel'. Early next morning we were back at the crossroads and on our way by 8.30 am, perched high up on oil drums in a battered old truck. We had grown so used to the forest pressing in on us on both sides of the dirt road that it came as quite a shock when we suddenly broke free of the trees and saw grassy hills rolling away into the distance. We could well imagine the relief and the raising of spirits Stanley's men must have experienced when, after so many months, they finally emerged from the dark forest into the sunlight. One of our fellow passengers proved quite knowledgeable about Stanley and pointed out a low hill on which he and his followers were said to have camped.

The outskirts of Bunia boasted several large, well-kept villas showing signs of European occupation and a big gilded Greek Orthodox church. The main street looked like a set for a 'wild west' town. Two-storey colonnaded wooden stores lined its long dusty expanse. All that was missing were the horses hitched to the rails. Bunia seemed more prosperous than many towns we had visited. Most of its shops were open for business and smartly painted. Its market was thriving. Permanent covered stalls were numbered and classified as to the type of goods on sale. One section specialised in sun-dried salted fish, another in fruit and vegetables, a third in dry goods such as salt and sugar, a fourth in clothes and a fifth in general goods. On the edge of the market were several butcher's shops, each displaying above the door a picture of the animal whose meat it sold. We counted three cows, one goat and a buffalo.

That first day we checked into the smart, newly-painted Hotel Semliki, and met the manager, Andreas Diamantidis, a Greek Cypriot whom we soon learnt had a brother living in Tottenham, north London, quite close to where John had

lived for many years. This was just another example of the 'small world' syndrome we have always found when travelling. Still eager to find some positive evidence of Stanley's expedition, we brought up the question of the plaque we had heard about.

'We've been told that there's an inscribed stone somewhere near here marking the site of Stanley's camp. Do you know where it is?' John asked.

'Oh yes,' Andreas replied. 'It used to stand at the crossroads outside the town. It was stolen about a year ago.'

Was there no escape from the bad luck dogging our footsteps? It seemed not.

Next morning was overcast and threatening rain as we set off for Kasenyi, the town some 2000 feet down the escarpment on the shores of Lake Albert, close to the spot where Stanley and the Advance Guard had first attempted, unsuccessfully, to make contact with Emin Pasha in December 1887. At the taxi station we found that all the vehicles for Kasenyi had left. This meant a five-mile walk to the crossroads (the very same from which the stone had been stolen) where the Kasenyi road turned off the main route, followed by a half-hour wait for a lift. This time we rode in style in the cab of a pick-up truck, for which we were very thankful as the track was steep, stony and extremely rough. At one point we came to a barrier lowered across the road. Here we waited while a man in a small stone-built hut telephoned down to his colleague at the other end to check if any vehicles were on the way up. They weren't, so the barrier was raised and we were allowed to continue. We were impressed by the efficiency of the system and especially by the fact that the telephone worked. We soon saw why the one-way system was needed. The road at this point resembled a narrow rocky river bed and plunged downhill at a terrifying angle.

Kasenyi was an unattractive, depressing little town of dilapidated warehouses, shacks and black dirt roads, but its appearance was deceptive. There was

obviously money around. Over a drink in a small bar, we met an English-speaking Zaïrean educated in Kampala, Uganda, who had worked for the government fisheries administration and was now in business on his own. 'I have four children at school in Belgium and one at the university in Kinshasa. I want him to go to university in England. Which do you think is better, Oxford or Cambridge?' he asked us. The dried fish business must have been doing rather well for him to be able to afford this kind of money for his children's education. But then Kasenyi was also a border point with Uganda, which could open up all sorts of profitable possibilities for a well-connected man.

We attempted to get some photographs of the lake, now officially known as Lake Mobutu Sese Seko after the president. This was more difficult than it seemed. The authorities would doubtless be highly sensitive about photographing such a 'strategic' point and we wanted to avoid more trouble. A narrow track through tall grass brought us down to the shore and a small fishing village of tumbledown shacks, surrounded by painted boats and fish laid out in the sun. In the water bobbed a collection of speedy-looking power boats, presumably the transport for more profitable trade with Uganda. The lake was a dirty grey under the heavy sky and looked distinctly uninviting. We were soon followed by a motley collection of children, adults, growling dogs and a couple of drunks, all of whom seemed surprised and less than delighted to see us there. It was not the ideal time or place to get out a camera. A second foray took us past the post office, the national flag and the immigration post to a wire fence by the port. No access to the lake that way. We finally snatched a few photos from behind a tall clump of grass while no one was looking. Not the best conditions for producing good pictures,

It was a dreary grey day when we eventually arrived on the shores of Lake Albert, where Stanley and Emin met for the first time on 29 April 1888.

but we had at least avoided being arrested. That task completed, we were more than ready to leave this unpleasant spot behind.

The journey back up to Bunia, on a load of smelly dried fish in the back of a pick-up truck, was quite hair-raising, but lightened by an incident just outside Kasenyi where the Collector of Regional Taxes had erected a road barrier. It was not clear whether this was official or a freelance operation, but in either case our driver was in no mood to pay taxes. Just before the barrier he suddenly dived off the road, drove at speed through a family compound, scattering chickens and cooking pots under his wheels and rejoined the road further on, leaving the official at the barrier shouting and gesticulating behind him. Stanley's departure from the lake was somewhat more dignified.

*****

At the end of their three weeks together, it was decided that Stanley would march off in search of Major Barttelot and the Rear Column, whilst Emin went to tour his provincial stations to canvass the views of his people. Mounteney Jephson was deputed to accompany the Pasha and to act as Stanley's representative. On 24 May 1888 the march commenced, Emin's band played them away, and Stanley was in action again. Stanley's confidence in the Pasha's authority over his people received a severe knock almost straight away. One hundred and twenty-nine native porters had been provided by Emin to make up for lost men, of whom at the end of the first day 110 ran away. Stanley's good humour was soon recovered when the clear weather conditions allowed him to confirm a sighting, made by Jephson and Parke about a month earlier, of snow-capped mountains. This was an exciting and important find, for what he saw was the Ruwenzori Mountain range, the fabled 'Mountains of the Moon'. The elusive prize sought by so many would go down as another entry on the long list of Stanley's discoveries.

By 8 June, the column was back at Fort Bodo, where everything was in good order. The acres of vegetable and fruit plantations were progressing well. Stairs had returned with the sick who had been left at Ugarrowwa's camp, but of the original 56, only 14 made it back to the fort. A week was spent in preparing for the next big effort, the relief of the Rear Column. Stairs, Nelson and Parke were to stay at the fort whilst Stanley, with a force of 213 volunteers, would again do battle with the forest. It had been arranged with Emin and Jephson that they would return in August, sending porters to Fort Bodo, which would then be abandoned, the camp transferred to Lake Albert and there they would await Stanley's arrival. Depending on where he found the Rear Column, Stanley expected to be back by December at the latest. A year had elapsed since he had left Yambuya, his promise to return in November 1887 forgotten. At least, Stanley hoped, the Major would be some way along the road towards him. It was now time to discover the truth.

The trail was well known, more use could be made of the river, and the expedition moved quickly west. In early August they caught up with the Arab Ugarrowwa, who was transferring his people down river to the Congo, and learnt that none of the dispatches sent to Major Barttelot had been delivered. On 17 August Stanley's flotilla of canoes started the descent of the wide sweep of river above the village of Banalya. Through binoculars, the expedition standard, the Egyptian flag, could be seen flying from the stockade. Stanley sprang to his feet: '"The Major, boys! Pull away bravely." A vociferous shouting and hurrahing followed, and every canoe shot forward at racing speed.'

The joy was to be short-lived. Waiting at the gate for them was William Bonny, alone. Stanley takes up the story:
'Pressing his hand, I said, "Well, Bonny, how are you? Where is the Major? Sick, I suppose?"

99

"The Major is dead, sir."

"Dead? Good God! How dead? Fever?"

"No, sir, he was shot."

"By whom?"

"By the Manyuema—Tippu Tip's people."

"Good heavens! Well, where is Jameson?"

"At Stanley Falls." [In fact, he died that same day in Bangala.]

"What is he doing there, in the name of goodness?"

"He went to obtain more carriers."

"Well then, where is Mr Ward or Mr Troup?"

"Mr Ward is at Bangala."

"Bangala! Bangala! what can he be doing there?"

"Yes, sir, he is at Bangala, and Mr Troup has been invalided home some months ago.'"

Stanley had found the Rear Column.

Inspecting the camp, Stanley found 'six dead bodies lying unburied, and the smitten living with their festers lounged in front of us by the dozen.' He was facing a disaster, compounded by the bitter story of the events of the last year poured out by the only European survivor to hand, William Bonny. But those were matters that must be pursued at some later date. The immediate problem was to salvage what remained of the Rear Column, get the men into some sort of shape and march them over 500 miles back through the forest to Lake Albert and the expedition's real task, the relief of Emin Pasha. First he must establish command and revive morale. He moved the whole caravan out of the charnel house of Banalya to an island six miles upstream to re-group. There, by sheer force of personality, Stanley, in a matter of two weeks, managed to turn the remnants of the Rear Column into a going concern.

On 31 August 1888 the expedition

Stanley finds the survivors of the Rear Column at Banalya.

100

marched east again. The roll call numbered 465:

Zanzibari carriers	210
(*including 45 sick*)	
Emin's men	61
Tippu Tip's men	61
Sudanese and Somalis	22
Camp followers	108
Europeans	3
Total	465

The march proceeded with most of the loads and sick men in canoes on the river, whilst the rest followed the forest trails. On 4 September Stanley received a visitor in camp, the nephew of Tippu Tip, and the man who had spent so long at Yambuya to the annoyance of Major Barttelot. Selim bin Mohammed came as the emissary of his uncle to establish whether Stanley blamed him for the Major's death. Stanley made it clear that he attached no blame to Tippu for Barttelot's murder, but that he would be holding him responsible for the Rear Column's delays and losses, a matter that would be taken up in the courts of law when they got to Zanzibar. This closed the association between Stanley and the Arab slave trader Tippu Tip. The next contacts would, indeed, be between their lawyers.

The 500-mile return journey to Fort Bodo was, as before, a desperate struggle against the twin perils of starvation and hostile natives. Hundreds were lost before the oasis in the forest was, at last, reached on 20 December. But all was not well. Emin Pasha and Jephson should have returned four months earlier, abandoned the fort and moved the camp to the lake to await Stanley's return as planned. There had been no sign, no word from either of them. Stanley had left them over seven months before. What could have gone wrong? If he had allowed himself such thoughts, Stanley must have been close to despair. So much had been endured, but nothing had yet been achieved. The Pasha was God knew where and the evacuation or relief of Equatoria was still no nearer than the day they had set sail from England.

Collapse of Equatoria

While Stanley was battling his way towards the relief of the Rear Column, Mounteney Jephson set out with Emin Pasha to tour his stations and assess the attitude of his men to the evacuation of the province. At this stage, Equatoria consisted of nine or ten stations stretching from M'swa on Lake Albert north along the Nile to Rejaf. Emin had under his nominal command about 1450 regular troops, split into two battalions and spread as garrisons over the various stations. These soldiers, and their officers, were mainly Sudanese. In addition, there were the irregular troops, natives drawn from a number of different tribal groups, who had proved to be the most effective of the fighting forces. Lastly, there were the Egyptians who made up the Civil Service and numbered about 65. Most officers, soldiers and clerks had large households with numerous wives, children, servants and slaves. These dependents constituted the bulk of the population of 8000–10,000 people.

At each station Jephson assembled the garrison and read to the men the Khedive's and Stanley's letters. He explained the implications of the options open to them and then tried to establish who wished to leave and who to stay. In these early encounters, the answer was always the same: 'If the Pasha stays we stay, if the Pasha goes we go.' But it was clear that the underlying desire was to stay. No mention was made of any alternative, other than staying where they were or returning to Egypt, but on three occasions officers suggested to Jephson that the best course would be to move to some other part of Africa where communications were better. Obviously word had already spread of Mackinnon's offer to Emin to establish a position to the north of Lake Victoria. Others were less enthusiastic about the offer and put quite a different interpretation on it. Two men who had been with Emin during his talks with Stanley started a campaign to discredit the latter and further undermine the Pasha's position. They wrote to other officers at the outlying stations, claiming that Stanley had not come from Egypt, that he was an impostor and adventurer, and that a secret plan had been hatched to sell them all into slavery under the British. These were stories that were to receive wide acceptance and place Jephson in considerable difficulties later.

From the beginning it was clear to Jephson that it would be no easy task to learn the true intentions of the Egyptians. They would bow and scrape and agree to everything to his face, but as soon as his back was turned would hatch plots and do the opposite of what had been decided. When they arrived at Emin's capital, Dufile, the station commander,

Hawashi Effendi, happily confirmed Jephson's suspicions with a little story: 'If a Soudanese comes at you with scowls and a loaded gun, whilst on the other hand an Egyptian comes to you with a carpet and a friendly salutation, turn to the Soudanese, he with his loaded gun will do you less harm.' Good advice from a man who was in a position to know. Hawashi had earned his banishment to Equatoria by selling his army's stores to the enemy during the war against the Abyssinians.

Dufile was at the head of steamer navigation between Lake Albert and the Nile. North of this point, rapids prevented the use of boats until the station at Lado was reached. Forming a caravan of 400 people, Emin and Jephson set out for the northern forts along the Nile. This would be a test of Emin's influence, as they were entering the region of the 1st Battalion, the soldiers who had defied the authority of the Pasha for the last four years. The rebels' headquarters was the station of Rejaf, the most northerly

Jephson intervenes to save the Pasha from his rebellious troops at Labore.

position still held, where they lived the life of robber barons, raiding the local tribes and living from their plunder. The caravan approached with caution. In mid-July, they halted at Kirri, two days' march from Rejaf, to gauge the mood of the soldiers. They opened negotiations by letter and were told to wait as no decisions could be taken until two of the rebel leaders returned from a patrol. Other news reached them via a spy that if Emin and Jephson came to the camp, it was intended to take them prisoner. In view of this intelligence, they decided to withdraw to the south. On leaving Kirri, the Pasha ordered that the ammunition from the station should follow him to prevent its falling into the hands of the rebels. On the road he heard that the soldiers had refused to follow his orders and had thrown in their lot with the men at Rejaf. Much to Jephson's disgust, Emin took no action to retrieve the situation and continued south.

On 12 August, Jephson made his speech to the men at the Labore station. It was met with disbelief and derision. Jephson was accused of lying. If the Khedive wanted to help them, why hadn't he sent an Egyptian officer? If the letter was genuine, it would be a command not a suggestion to do 'as you please', and if Jephson had come from Egypt, why didn't he come carrying letters from their families? These were quite reasonable questions that did not have satisfactory answers. When Emin tried to take control and discipline the men an ugly scene followed and both Europeans were, for a time, in danger of being shot. Jephson managed, bravely, to quieten the men long enough to allow his party to move on. By 14 August they were at the small station of Char Ayu, where they received word from Dufile that the garrison there had gone over to the rebels. They were trapped. With rebellious troops to both north and south, there was no option but

104

Emin and Jephson ride into Dufile to face arrest by the rebels.

to go on to Dufile and face it out. Tension was high as they entered the town. Silent crowds watched them make their slow progress to the main square. There, soldiers manhandled them from their donkeys and bundled them into Emin's compound. They were now under house arrest, at the mercy of the whims of a mutinous army.

The dissident officers had formed a council to act as their governing body and to decide on future policy. This turned into an endless talking shop, sitting for weeks and deciding on little other than their personal promotions. On 3 September, Jephson accompanied a crowd of officers and men on a visit to the stations of Wadelai and Tunguru. The trip gave him the opportunity to send messages south through one or two officers who

had remained loyal, alerting Stanley to the situation when he eventually returned to the lake. Back at Dufile, he continued his vigil with the Pasha.

In mid-October news came that was to force the issue and change the situation dramatically. It was reported that after an absence of four years, the Mahdi's army had returned in force and had landed at the abandoned station of Lado. With the province again under threat, confusion reigned. Hurried arrangements were made to try to reinforce the garrison at Rejaf, but early in November the station fell. A column was sent to re-take it, but this in turn was routed by the Dervish soldiers of the Mahdi. All the northern stations were abandoned and the army consolidated on Dufile to await the onslaught. Every day, refugees came pouring into the town and were dispatched further south on the steamers. The fact that the collapse of the province had coincided with the deposing of the Pasha was not lost on the common soldiers. They rose against the officers' council and forced the release of Emin and Jephson. The officers came cap in hand to Emin, begging him to resume the governorship, but Emin by this time seems to have come to the conclusion that Equatoria was lost and that there was nothing more he could do for it. He refused to accept responsibility and joined the refugees moving south. By 17 November Emin and Jephson were at Wadelai station awaiting developments.

All was quiet for about two weeks, then, on 4 December, messengers came from Dufile with news that the Mahdi had triumphed. Wadelai was only one day's sail from Dufile. They would have to move fast. With no boat available to them, they would have to make their way overland to the lake. Next morning Emin and Jephson marched from Wadelai at the head of a long and ragged band of refugees. Emin's people were unused to marching and were encumbered with useless possessions which they refused to leave behind. Before the end of the first day, two-thirds of the refugees had given up the struggle and returned to the station, preferring to take their chances with the Mahdi.

The column progressed a little more smoothly with the smaller numbers until, on 7 December, one of the steamers was seen approaching. If it was the Mahdi's soldiers, they had no chance, but as it drew closer it was clear that it was Emin's own people. It transpired that Dufile had not fallen. In fact, more by luck than judgement, the Dervish hordes had been repulsed and were retreating north in disarray. The captain of the boat was persuaded to transport Emin and his followers to the next station to the south, Tunguru. Here Emin established himself and adopted his 'wait and see' mode.

The Mahdi's army had not given up

and gone home. It had simply fallen back on Rejaf and sent for reinforcements from Khartoum. It would only be a temporary respite before the storm broke again. The rebel officers abandoned Dufile and retreated to the more defensible position at Wadelai. There they reconvened the council to carry on doing what it did best, talking.

The next development was the receipt of reliable news that Stanley had arrived back at Kavalli's, at the southern end of Lake Albert. By 28 January 1889, Jephson had managed to get himself as far as M'swa by steamer, Emin having decided to stay on at Tunguru for the time being. He was still having great difficulty in making the final break from the province for which he had laboured for so long. There always seemed to be a distant hope that maybe, by some miracle, all would come right again and he would be able to stay on. Jephson had no such illusions and was hurrying to rendezvous with Stanley before he got left behind. Stanley had specified that he would wait only until 6 February. It was already 31 January, and now Jephson had to descend the lake by canoe. Despite bad weather, he arrived on 5 February with a day to spare. After eight months away, he was welcomed warmly. Guns were fired off, men rushed up to shake his hand and Stanley calmly added his own welcome home. Jephson wrote: 'I think he was pleased to see me again, I know I was glad to see him.' The untried dilettante had won his spurs.

On 12 February Emin arrived at the lake shore, accompanied by a deputation of officers and the first batch of refugees. The officers had decided to come to see Stanley to assess the forces he had at his disposal. They had assumed that he would refuse to meet them unless Emin was with them and had therefore asked the Pasha to accompany them as interpreter. When Emin refused this role, the officers reluctantly agreed he could be Pasha again. The title was meaningless, but at least Emin could present himself before Stanley with some semblance of dignity and an apparent following. So it was agreed they go to Stanley, but it was still far from decided if they would condescend to be rescued.

The Pasha, accompanied by the deputation of officers, met with Stanley on 18 February. Stanley outlined his purpose in coming to the lake and enquired if the officers intended to stay put or to follow him to the coast. No other options were discussed and the deputation professed that their hearts' desire was to return to Egypt. All they asked was to be given sufficient time to gather their people and bring them down the lake, a request to which Stanley agreed. Having learnt from Jephson the true situation in Equatoria, he had evidently come to the conclusion that his dreams of establishing sovereignty for King Leopold, or of carrying out Sir William Mackinnon's plans, were quite impractical. On the other hand, simply to deliver the 'relief' supplies that had cost so much suffering would be futile. The Pasha had no power or following and the supplies would do no more than bolster a rebel army. There was no choice. Stanley would have to take Emin, and any of his people who chose to accompany him, to the coast. This complete change of plan was forced on Stanley by circumstances. Little more than a month earlier, he had told his officers that to escort a large caravan to the coast was an impossibility in view of the small number of men left under his command. He would now have to attempt that impossible mission.

Emin's officers did not make a good impression. The expedition doctor described them as: 'licentious, indolent, over-fed, bloated, congested masses of human flesh.' Their untrustworthy nature was confirmed when, on departure, one of the officers stole a rifle. Stanley learnt the further galling fact that he would be leaving a vast store of wealth in the hands of these good-for-nothings. On his tour of the province, Jephson had inspected the ivory stores at the stations and had taken the trouble to calculate the ivory's worth at the coast. It came to the staggering figure of £112,250, which would have paid for all the expedition expenses five times over. As Jephson noted: 'All this ivory would have to be abandoned, as we could never carry it to the coast. It was grievous that so much money should have to be thrown away.' The existence of this treasure would obviously ease the pain of having to give up years of back pay for those who chose to stay in Equatoria.

The expedition was now gathered in camp. Stairs, Nelson and Parke had arrived with the invalids and the remaining loads to join Jephson, Bonny and Stanley. Over the next few weeks, a steady stream of refugees reached the lake, together with huge amounts of baggage. The expedition officers, assisted by large contingents of their native allies, busied themselves in organising the transport of what was described as 'rubbish' up the steep escarpment to the camp, a labour which put a severe strain on the goodwill of the officers and Zanzibari porters.

The date for departure had been set for 10 April 1889, despite further pleas to extend the date from various tardy officers and from Emin himself. The Pasha was still confident that most of his men would follow him out in the end. To Stanley, this was nonsense. The requests for delay he considered a ruse to allow the rebels to organise and make an attack on the camp to steal the ammunition. By the end of March, 1355 loads had been transported to the camp and about 600 of Emin's people had assembled. Of these, only about 50 were soldiers or clerks, the rest being family and servants. Emin was still fretting over his decision to leave. His friend, Casati, had been trying to persuade him that his duty lay with 'his people'. Stanley was not slow to point out to the Pasha that he had been abandoned by his people and his only reward for staying would be imprisonment and execution. His duty now was to take those who wished to the coast. A few days later, poor Emin was to discover the degree of loyalty

that he commanded. Calling his household of personal servants and assistants together, he asked who would go to the coast with him. Out of 51 of those closest to him, only four said they would follow him. The truth was beginning to dawn.

On 5 April, word came to Stanley that attempts had been made by Emin's men to steal the expedition's guns. Stanley saw this as the culmination of the plotting that was endemic amongst the Egyptians, and with just five days to go before the start of the march, it was time to exert some authority. The Pasha was called to his presence and asked what he proposed to do. When it became clear that he would prefer to follow his usual principle of 'wait and see', Stanley informed him: 'In my camp indiscipline and unruliness shall not prevail.' With that, he marched

out to take control of the situation. A parade was called. Emin's people took no notice and had to be forced out of their huts. There followed a Stanley 'set piece' in which he made a stirring speech, identified and imprisoned the main dissidents and got the assembled mass to declare their ardent desire to follow him to the ends of the earth. Stanley was now in command. All pretence that the Pasha had any standing was dropped, the only official role now left to him being expedition naturalist and meteorologist.

On the morning of 10 April 1889, the march to the coast began. Behind them the expedition was leaving the ruins of Equatoria province. The relief they had delivered had fallen into the hands of the rebel officers, but they still held the bulk of the ammunition and goods brought

Stanley takes command of Emin's followers.

108

up from Yambuya. The plan to provide Emin with the supplies that would have allowed him to make a free choice regarding his future actions had failed. Events had overtaken them and closed off all options except one, the march to the sea. As the caravan made its slow progress across the rolling hills, Stanley estimated his force at 1510 people. About 550 of these were native bearers provided by the local chiefs; the Pasha had a following of some 600 people; of the original expedition, 230 men remained alive; of Tippu Tip's men, 130 still followed Stanley.

It was now more than two years since the expedition had landed at Banana Point at the mouth of the Congo River. In that time, Stanley had covered about 4800 miles. Between him and the east coast lay a march of over 1200 miles. He had grave doubts that many of the Pasha's people would make it to the sea.

Mountains of the Moon

Just three days into the march, Stanley was taken seriously ill with a recurrence of the sickness that had laid him low a few months earlier at Fort Bodo. Everything ground to a halt to await his recovery. This delay would give ample opportunity for any of Emin's people who chose to catch up with the expedition. The effect was quite the contrary. Those who had started out began to drift away. As far as Stanley was concerned, he was well rid of them, until one of them committed the crime that he never tolerated, the stealing of rifles. A man named Rehan, together with 22 others, had made off with a number of guns. Stairs was dispatched to retrieve the man and the weapons. On his return Rehan was tried by the expedition officers and sentenced to death. Unusually, Stanley was against this drastic action, but eventually bowed to the majority view. Still very weak, he insisted on struggling from his bed to pass sentence. In attempting to deliver one of his orations to the masses, he fell to the ground in his debilitated state, but persevered and saw the man hanged at the second attempt.

During this period of enforced rest, Emin's people were as active as ever in their favoured pastimes of plotting and treachery. At one stage, the Pasha actually stirred himself to try one man and sentenced him to death for treason. He sent to Stanley for a firing squad, only to be told that he should deal with the matter himself. Unable to find any of his own people willing to carry out his orders, Emin was forced to spare the man's life. From that point, he lost interest in trying to exert authority and buried himself in his private world of beetles, bugs, birds and flowers. Stanley's servant, Hoffman, found Emin's lack of interest inexplicable:

While Stanley was tossing in delirium and while plots and counter plots were carried out beneath our very eyes, the chief figure of the Relief Expedition, Emin Pasha, pottered happily about the camp, adding to his collection of birds and insects. . . . His gallant rescuer might be dying, his men might desert him, but bring him a rare bird, an unknown beetle, a strange flower, and he would immediately become wrapped in a sort of divine ecstasy from which it was impossible to rouse him.

The whole of April passed in camp with Stanley too ill to move. Then in May he began to recover. On 3 May, he interested himself in the affairs of the camp during his illness, to find that there were still men plotting to overthrow him and take the ammunition. Letters were intercepted which clearly showed that a force of rebels was expected to arrive at any time. On 8 May, the caravan lumbered into action again and resumed the march. The night before it left, 25 cases of ammunition were secretly buried to relieve the porters of the loads and, possibly, to remove an incentive for trouble from the rebel officers.

Through May, the column made its slow progress south, following a route along the wide Rift Valley close to the Semliki River, with the huge, mist-shrouded bulk of the Ruwenzori Mountains to its left. The going was relatively easy as they moved through open grasslands and occasional patches of woodland near the river. As they had now left the area controlled by Stanley's native allies, irregular skirmishes occurred with the local tribes, but more usually the tribesmen simply stood on distant hills and watched the caravan pass. It was known that the forces of the powerful King Kabba Rega were raiding in the area of the Semliki Valley. Kabba Rega's kingdom lay to the east of Lake Albert and along the foothills of the Ruwenzori range, but he had a large army, well armed with muskets, which extended his rule over a much wider area. On 18 May,

the caravan was engaged in crossing to the east bank of the Semliki, a dangerous operation which took two days to accomplish as only two canoes could be found. Whilst in this exposed position, they came under fire from a party of 50 or 60 of Kabba Rega's troops. No damage was done and the soldiers were effectively chased away, but it seemed probable that this was just the scouting party for a major force further off. They would have to be on their guard. The days of friendly receptions were over. The river crossing provided an opportunity to take a count of the column's numbers. There were 1168 men, women and children, 610 loads, 235 head of cattle and some sheep and goats.

After the river crossing, conditions became more difficult when they found themselves travelling through forest. Stanley was proceeding with exceptional care, in deference to the large number of women and children in the column. A day's march was rarely more than two or three hours, but even so the Pasha's people complained constantly of the terrible burden placed on them. Emin

The expedition comes under attack while crossing the Semliki River.

111

was no better. His collecting had become a mania and he pressed for more rest days. Stanley was becoming exasperated. He wrote bitterly of the slatternly habits of the Egyptians, of the scores of crying babies keeping him awake at night, and of Emin he wrote: 'He would slay every bird in Africa; he would collect ugly reptiles, and every hideous insect; he would gather every skull until we should become a travelling museum and cemetery.' Stanley did not have much time for these natural history activities, believing that his geographical surveys of this previously untravelled area would be of more lasting benefit to the world than any number of stuffed birds. Perhaps not surprisingly, the relationship between the two men had been on the decline since the Pasha's last vestiges of power had been usurped by Stanley back in April, an act that Stanley knew full well Emin would hold against him: 'As long as life lasts, he will hold me

in aversion.' He was already starting to worry that it would be Emin's querulous account of affairs that would be accepted when they returned to Europe.

The expedition found, to its great relief, that the region was rich in food, unlike the Ituri Forest. The problems of feeding the caravan were few, so Stanley was able to stop for a time to investigate the mysteries of the Mountains of the Moon. They had been traversing the foothills for some time and had come to a point that semed to offer a route deeper into the mountains. It was now Lieutenant Stairs' turn to find a place in the history books. As the only man fit and willing, it was he who attempted to become the first European to climb the Ruwenzori peaks. On 6 June he set out, accompanied by a group of Zanzibaris keen to investigate snow. Initially, the Pasha went with them, but had to return after a climb of 1000 feet. Stairs did better,

Lieutenant Stairs attempted the first ascent of the Ruwenzori Mountains, discovered by the expedition.

reaching a height of about 10,500 feet, but was then forced back through lack of time and the effects of the unfamiliar cold on the Zanzibaris. He went far enough to get a good view of the snow peaks and to discover sufficiently ususual plant specimens to keep Emin happy. Stairs made his entry into the mountains about 20 miles north of what, in later years, was to prove the easiest route from the village of Mutwanga.

By mid-June, the expedition had reached the southern end of the mountain range and turned its course to the west. From a promontory, Stanley caught sight of a second large lake, to be called confusingly the Albert Edward, later simply known as Lake Edward. This was an important discovery as it effectively solved the mystery of the Nile sources, a subject that constituted the main geographical argument of the nineteenth century. What Stanley had established was that the Semliki River flowed from Lake Edward to Lake Albert and that therefore Edward was a primary source. He had seen the snows of the fabled Mountains of the Moon, defined their position and confirmed their role as the Central African watershed feeding the Nile. In geographical terms the expedition was an assured success.

*****

Now it was time for us to follow Stanley south, our main objective on this leg of the journey, the Ruwenzori Mountains, so different from the other snow-caps of east central Africa, Mount Kilimanjaro and Mount Kenya. The latter rise clearly visible from the surrounding plains, isolated white cones in the tropical landscape. The Ruwenzori range, rising from forested foothills, is rarely visible, almost constantly shrouded in cloud and mist.

We intended to begin our ascent of the mountains from the village of Mutwanga. To get there we had to retrace our steps to the crossroads at Komanda and from there take the road to Beni, the nearest big town to the mountain base camp.

John was still keen to make contact with pygmies, as they figured in Stanley's accounts and a few had even accompanied his party on the journey to East Africa. He brought the subject up just before our departure from Bunia.

'Before we leave the area, why don't we make one last attempt to visit a pygmy group?' he suggested.

'Fine,' I replied warily, 'so long as you're not proposing to go back to the mission at Lolwa.' The thought of retracing a stage of the journey which had taken us so long to accomplish was not attractive. 'Good heavens, no,' said John hastily. 'I'm talking about Mount Hoyo. According to the map there's a turn off to it 12 km [7½ miles] down the Beni road from Komanda. We could do the round trip in a few days.'

Mount Hoyo was a forested mountain retreat that had been a favourite weekend spot for Belgian colonials. They had built a lodge there, attracted by the climate and the beauty of the area, the series of magnificent caves in the limestone cliffs and the tumbling waterfall known as the Venus Staircase. But more important, from our point of view, was that a pygmy settlement was located there. It was decided. Our next port of call would be Beni, with a side trip to Mount Hoyo. Now all we needed to do was get there.

Andreas, at the Semliki Hotel, provided the unlikely information that a weekly bus service plied the route between Bunia and Beni and that it was due to go the next morning. It even had a name, the *Butembo Safari*. Well, if this was true then perhaps our luck was taking a turn for the better. Indeed, it was true. The bus was ancient, it was rickety, its roof looked in imminent danger of collapse under the weight of baggage it was carrying, but it had seats with only one passenger to each and it was a good deal more comfortable than sitting on an oil drum in the back of a lorry. We could have got off at the Mount Hoyo turning but we had decided, as there would be no passing traffic on the road to the lodge, to try to hire a pick-up truck in Komanda to take us all the way. Of course there was absolutely nothing for hire in Komanda when we left the bus and we ended up getting a ride on a lorry to the turn-off, a journey we could have accomplished more easily, quickly and cheaply by staying on the bus.

No sooner had the lorry driven away than a small elderly man of mixed Bantu and pygmy blood, who lived in a hut at the road junction, set about getting us organised.

'You want to go to Mount Hoyo? How many bags have you got?' He counted them. Two rucksacks and a small but heavy holdall.

'My two sons can carry the big bags. My grandson can carry the small bag, but his brother must go with him to help.'

We were more than happy to agree, as the little lad in question only looked about seven. His helper was even smaller. Our intention had been to wait for a lift, but the old man was such an efficient organiser that within ten minutes our bags were being toted up the mountain track and we were running to keep up with them. In fact it was just as well we didn't wait for transport. There were no other guests at the lodge during the two days we were there and the register showed an average of only one set of visitors per week. The eight-mile climb started out quite gently, passing a couple of small Bantu villages where people called out friendly greetings, but got steeper and hotter as time went by.

After three hours, we finally panted out of the forest on to the lawn of the *Auberge de Mont Hoyo*. What a delightful place. Chalets, each containing four double rooms, were scattered around the extensive grounds. The bar, restaurant and reception were in a separate building and the terrace behind them overlooked a luxuriously blossoming garden cut out of the lush green forest. Far beyond and below, the Ituri Forest rolled away into the mist. We could have stayed a week, it was so lovely. The only drawback was we couldn't afford to stay a week. We compromised and settled for two nights. That evening we were served wild mushrooms at dinner. They looked like small white strips of spaghetti and tasted delicious. The waiter told us that the pygmies gathered them in the forest. Later, we learnt that they came from the 'plantations' of leaf cutter ants which build up piles of leaves underground and cultivate the fungus as food. We were glad we didn't know the history of them when we ate them.

Next morning we were taken in hand by the park guide (Mount Hoyo is part of Zaïre's national park system) and set off to see the sights. First of all, the Matupi grotto where the guide lit his powerful Tilly lamp and led us through a series of caves, some low and narrow, others huge and vaulted. In one, bats hung from the ceiling, in others, stalagmites formed strange ghostly shapes in the flickering lamplight: a gnarled old oak tree, a waterfall, piano keys that sounded eerily when struck with a stone. This was only a small section of the caves that riddle Mount Hoyo. Back at the lodge, an old map showed the many grottoes that still remain to be explored.

From the Matupi grotto, our guide took us to a small river, the Issehe, and the *Escalier de Vénus*, the pretty Venus Staircase waterfall. A fault in the rock formation has created a series of steps, about 30 feet high, over which the little river tumbles down into an almost perfectly round pool fringed by graceful palms. You could believe that you had stumbled on a secret grove in the Garden of Eden, a sanctuary hidden away from the rough and ready world of Central Africa.

On our return from the waterfall, we were approached by the chief of the pygmy village, a sinewy elderly man wearing a civet skin round his neck and a barkcloth loincloth. He invited us to visit his village that afternoon and witness traditional dancing. He named quite a high price. It seemed that the Mount Hoyo

The 'Venus Staircase', one of the attractions to be seen at Mount Hoyo.

pygmies were well and truly commercialised. As the main purpose of our visit was to make contact with a pygmy group, we agreed, although this wasn't quite the contact we had had in mind. Comments in the lodge's visitors' book were less than encouraging. The dancing, which was obviously a regular option for guests, was described variously as 'boring' and a 'rip off'.

When we visited the village and saw the dances for ourselves, we totally disagreed. No doubt those who wrote the comments were expecting to see the exuberant, colourful, athletic dances, accompanied by powerful drumming, that are associated with the Bantu tribes of black Africa. Their expectations were false. Pygmy dances represent in mime form events of daily life: hunting elephant, baboon and chimpanzees, catching freshwater crabs, the marriage ritual. The old chief sat on a stool, beating out a rhythm with hand and stick on a skin-covered drum, whilst the dancers circled around him, stamping their feet and chanting. It was true that at first they appeared simply to be going through the motions, but soon the spirit of the dance absorbed them and they all laughed as loudly as we did at the antics of the 'chimpanzees', the 'baboons', and the two young girls with toes and fingers intertwined who mimed the river crabs. When they heard the sound of the drum and laughter, a crowd from the Bantu village nearby quickly gathered to enjoy the dances. We felt our money had been well spent. It provided a wonderful afternoon's entertainment for everyone. Not so welcome was the insistent importuning by pygmy women and children when the

The pygmy chief prepares to provide the accompaniment for the dancing at his Mount Hoyo village.

116

Pygmy dances are an extension of story telling and depict events from life, such as hunting trips and the antics of the animals of the forest. These girls imitate the movements of fresh-water crabs in the crab dance.

dancing was finished and we were on our way out of the leaf hut village, but then nothing's ever perfect. It seemed that the pygmy peoples have been astonishingly successful at exploiting the modern world that encroaches on them, taking what they want from it, but still maintaining their traditional life-style.

We enjoyed our last evening on the verandah, gazing out over the flame trees and mimosa in the sloping garden to the tall forest beyond, where black mangabeys leapt through the branches. Our brief holiday—for that was how it felt— over, we hired three cheerful young men from the local village to carry our equipment and set off down the mountain. On the way we passed several of yesterday's dancers.

'Bonjour. Jambo,' they called out to us. Their faces, serious in repose, were quite transformed by their friendly smiles.

Although our contact with them had been slight and superficial, we liked the BaMbuti—as they called themselves— and would have liked to know them better. Their knowledge and love of the forest and the plants and creatures that lived in it was legendary, much superior to that of the Bantu who ventured into the trackless heart of the forest only when forced to.

Soon we were back on a bumpy pick-up truck and on our way to Beni. The road was generally good, as it was still the dry season, and we were there in three hours. The town looked prosperous. There were new buildings, well-maintained stores and a smart hotel on the paved main street. This was an area of plantations: tea, coffee, cocoa and cinchona, from which quinine is produced. It had altitude and a good climate on its side and had always been a favourite area with the

117

Belgian colonials for living, working and holidaying.

At lunch-time on the verandah of the Hotel Beni, we met a group of 16 English tourists with their driver. They were on a three-week safari in eastern Zaïre, taking in an ascent of the Ruwenzori Mountains and a visit to the mountain gorillas. They travelled in a big Bedford truck fitted out with benches in the back and slept in tents at night. They, like us, were heading for the mountain base camp next day. The thought of trekking up the mountain paths and spending nights in the mountain huts with a large, noisy group did not appeal to us. We had got out of the habit of coping with so many English speakers all at once. We decided to get away really early in the morning and try to reach the base camp at Mutsora in time to set off up the mountain the same day. We hoped this would give us at least a day's lead over the group.

Our plan didn't work. There was no transport to be had until 8.30 am and we arrived at Mutsora, 31 miles away, two hours later. By this time it was too late to organise the necessary porters.

'We'll leave early tomorrow morning,' Kanyunzu promised. 'Today you can get together your permits and I'll organise a group of porters.'

Kanyunzu was an old friend, an English-speaking Zaïrean who had grown up in Uganda. He was a National Park guide and had led us on the mountain two years before, when we had taken a small group of Americans on safari. They were not very fit and we had not managed to get beyond the second hut at just under 11,000 feet. This time we were determined to get to the top on our own.

We knew there were a few people ahead of us on the mountain, but we were the only ones at the base camp that day. We sat on the rocks by the rushing river and watched darting wagtails. The place looked smarter than we remembered. The National Park office and the director's office were well maintained, the block of visitors' rooms basic but clean

and the grass neatly cut. The National Parks organisation, in Kivu Region at least, was one of the few things that ran with smooth efficiency. In the gardens surrounding the camp, planted many years ago by Belgians, a fine collection of trees and shrubs, many flowering exuberantly, provided shade and elegance. The dark forest-clad foothills of the Ruwenzori formed the backdrop to this scene, but from here one had no

Renzaho Barizira, usually known as Apolline, runs the administration of the Ruwenzori base camp at Mutsora with firm efficiency.

118

idea of the snow-capped peaks that lay beyond.

Next morning Kanyunzu arrived with our four porters, two to carry our equipment, one to act as the water bearer (there is no water at the huts and it has to be carried up from rivers *en route*) and the fourth man to carry the porters' food. No one is allowed on the mountain without a guide and porters, and their fees are set by the park authorities. There is an entrance fee to the park, which includes the guide, then a small amount for the use of the huts. The porters are paid at a standard rate per day, settled at the end, plus a charge for their food, paid in advance. The Banande, the local people, have been employed as porters ever since European climbers first became interested in the range at the turn of the century. The first to reach the summit of Mount Stanley, Margherita peak at 16,763 feet, was an Italian aristocrat and mountaineer, Prince Luigi Amedeo of Savoy, the Duke of the Abruzzi, in 1906. Mount Emin's summit is lower than Mount Stanley's, as Stanley would no doubt have considered fitting, at 15,740 feet, and there are even two peaks named after our own Royal

family, Elizabeth at 16,170 feet, and Philip at 16,140 feet.

When we reached the village of Mutwanga, where the climb begins, four miles from the Mutsora camp, we met up with the overland group who had camped overnight in the grounds of a derelict hotel (it was in the process of being refurbished, but seemed to have made little progress since we had last seen it two years before). We knew they would have a couple of hours' hassle ahead of them as the porters sorted out their loads, and we wanted to get away before them. But it was Saturday, *salongo* day, the shops did not open until 11 am, and we needed to buy supplies. We decided to delegate this task to Kanyunzu and set off along the path. We had no need of a guide and knew that the porters were sure to overtake us before we reached the first hut. This section of the climb, from base camp at 3900 feet to Hut 1 at 6700 feet, was reckoned to take six hours. The tough, barefoot porters, carrying heavy loads, raced up in about two hours, so didn't bother leaving very early. Instead, they normally entertained themselves with a drink or three in Mutwanga before

The thickly wooded foothills of the Ruwenzori Mountains from Hut 1.

setting off with assorted bags slung from rattan bands across their foreheads.

The path rose steeply through an area of cultivated gardens and compounds for an hour and a half. There was little shade and the sun was fierce. We were thankful to plunge into the cool dimness of the forest which started abruptly where the cultivation finished. The path was clear and not too muddy. The trees were dense, but not giants like those that grew at lower altitudes and there were many flowering shrubs, climbers and herbaceous plants. Being alone, we saw several birds—regal sunbirds, white-necked ravens and a Ruwenzori turaco—and heard chimpanzees hooting in the distance. A big group of black and white Ruwenzori colobus monkeys jumped and shrieked overhead as we sat eating our lunch.

We reached Kalonge Hut, at 6700 feet, after a five and a half-hour climb. We had seen nothing of the porters. The overlanders began to straggle in and finally, after dark, a band of sheepish porters arrived. Evidently, the imbibing at the village had gone on longer than usual. Their food supply, a live pig, appeared tied to a pole carried between two men. The porters' meal of roast pork that evening was considerably more lavish and appetising than our offering of dehydrated mush. Soon after the meal, we all retired to our sleeping bags, a few on wooden bedsteads, the rest on the floor. It was a tight fit with 18 people squeezed into the three-roomed hut.

Next morning, we were away early and had soon left the montane forest and passed into the bamboo zone. One of the strange features of these equatorial mountains is the dramatic change that takes place in the vegetation at certain well-defined altitudes. Towards the end of the day's climb, the bamboo and

Kanyunzu, our mountain guide, in the lichen-covered forest approaching Hut 2. RIGHT

Fallen trees, deep mud and rocks thickly coated in sphagnum mosses are a feature of the route to Hut 2. BELOW RIGHT

Porters move ahead, making their way through the moss forest above Hut 1. BELOW LEFT

tangled undergrowth came to an end and the heather took over. This was not the low bush that grows on English uplands. These were tree heathers growing to a height of 20 to 30 feet and festooned with grey-green mosses and lichens. Their exposed roots were cushioned in hummocks of sphagnum moss whose colours ranged from vivid green through yellow to reddish-gold. Clouds hung low over the tops of the trees. We felt cut off in a strange, colourful dream world, but we could only appreciate its beauty when we stopped to rest. Our attention had to be concentrated on the steep trail in front of us. Once in the heather zone, it had become muddy. Exposed roots tripped the unwary and low branches cracked the careless climber over the head. As we rose higher, *Disa stairsii*, an orchid with a

spike of coral-pink flowers, began to appear. We were glad that Lieutenant Stairs' ascent of the mountains had achieved recognition in the naming of this pretty flower. It was also notable as the only tangible connection we had found with Stanley's expedition. We reached Mahangu hut at 10,936 feet after five and a half hours. We had now overtaken Stairs, who had had to abandon his attempt at 10,600 feet. We had been climbing in cloud all day, but in the late afternoon the clouds suddenly cleared and gave us a marvellous view of the snow peaks ahead and the Semliki plain below, backed by the long line of the Mitumba Mountains.

It was 3 August, our wedding anniversary. We had a celebratory meal of corned beef, baked beans and a bottle of red wine. Even out of plastic cups it tasted good. The claret had been one of the free gifts left in our suite at the Inter-Continental in Kinshasa, way back in June, and we had been carrying it around with us ever since. It was some sort of miracle that it had survived to be enjoyed at Hut 2 on the Ruwenzori Mountains. As the wind whistled around the hut, the temperature dropped to near freezing and the candles sputtered, the somewhat depleted English contingent settled into the familiar activities of home. They held a meeting. This entertaining discussion was called to air the grievances and complaints that they planned to make to their tour leader, Robin, who had sensibly stayed down in Mutwanga on the pretext of having work to do on the truck. Having led various tours ourselves, we found

A rare clear view of the Ruwenzori snow peaks, taken in the early morning en route *to Hut 3. In this region, groundsel grows as a tree and St John's Wort as a bush.* ABOVE

Hut 3, Kiondo, at 14,119 ft (4200 m) with the peaks hidden in their mantle of cloud. ABOVE RIGHT

A tantalising glimpse of the snows of Ruwenzori as the clouds swirl around the peaks. BELOW RIGHT

122

it amusing and instructive to see the other side of the coin.

After a couple of hours' climb next day, we emerged into the alpine zone, a strange land where the English country garden seems to have gone wild. Familiar names such as lobelia, St John's wort, everlastings and groundsel proliferate, but are unrecognisable as those well-behaved plants from home. The blue-flowered spikes of the lobelias grow to a height of 12 feet, giant groundsels stand like sentinels in an alien landscape, trees of orange-flowering St John's wort dot the slopes and *Helichrysum* everlastings grow in thick bushes 4 or 5 ft high, their creamy-white flowers closing in the rain and opening in the sun.

Kiondo hut, at 14,119 feet, was built of

Lac Gris, close to Hut 3, with a giant groundsel and Helichrysum *everlastings in the foreground.*

In the evenings, the clouds hang like smoke in the valleys.

stone and had a fire burning when we arrived. Its only residents were two porters who were guarding the baggage of an American climbing party up on the glaciers. A few of the overlanders made it to Hut 3 and the really athletic amongst them, including the youngest and oldest in the party, went straight up to the peak of Mount Mugule before descending to Hut 2 to spend the night. We could take our time. We planned for a day longer on the mountain than their schedule allowed.

After a very cold night, during which a gale-force wind howled around and through the hut, we made the climb up to Wasuwameso peak at 14,725 feet, the summit of Mount Mugule, the westerly neighbour of Mount Stanley. If you are equipped for snow and ice work, it is possible to climb to a fourth hut and from there explore the main mountain range, but for us Wasuwameso was as high as we could safely go.

The morning was clear, crisp and beautiful. At the summit we stood silent before the Gods of the Ruwenzori, the rocky masses of snow peaks that rose before us in powerful majesty. Their names, provided mainly by European royalty and aristocracy, seemed inadequate titles to express the grandeur of their existence: Albert, Margherita, Alexandra, Moebius, Elena, Tooth Edge, Savoia, Elizabeth and Philip. It was a place that demanded deeper thoughts. As we watched, the sun rose dazzlingly behind the Moebius Glacier and flashed brilliant rays over the mountain's hunched shoulder. It was a moment that made all the struggles worthwhile, a moment of rare privilege. We tore ourselves away. Soon the clouds would sweep in again and down below by the hut, we could see the tiny figures of Kanyunzu and our porters, reminders that it was time to return to the world of mere mortals.

We had decided to spend the night

125

Dawn breaks over the summit ridge of Margherita, 16,790 ft (5119 m), the highest of the Ruwenzori peaks.

Looking back towards the Semliki plain, a part of the Rift Valley.

The occasional chimpanzee call or the rushing of a stream are the only noises that encroach on the silent forests of Ruwenzori.

at the first hut, Kalonge, a descent of 7,400 feet. All went well until we reached Hut 2, when the relentless downward pressure began to take its toll and our knees turned to jelly. When we put a foot down we felt as though we had no control over the knee joint, as though it might bend backwards just as easily as forwards. It took us nine hours to crawl down to Kalonge.

We were in no better shape the following day on the descent to Mutwanga, taking five hours against our porters' one and a half. The gale we had heard blowing two nights before had caused havoc in the forest. Many trees had fallen across the path and we had to detour round them, Kanyunzu slashing at foliage with his machete. From Mutwanga we hobbled the last few painful miles to Mutsora and the base camp, where it was pay day for the porters. The ritual was that in addition to their basic pay, they received a bonus and any items of clothing that climbers no longer required. We duly parted with our money and T-shirts and a small watch for Kanyunzu, which seemed to please him greatly.

After five days on foot in the rarefied atmosphere of the mountains, we were back to dirt roads and the unending search for transport along them. This was the last lap of our journey in Zaïre. Our

objective now was the border town of Kasindi and, beyond it, Uganda. Next morning we walked into Mutwanga with Kanyunzu to look for a lorry. We were dismayed to see large numbers of soldiers lounging about on the main street and making trouble in the market. Over a drink in one of the bars, we learnt that the soldiers were camped in the grounds of the old hotel and were in action against rebels in the hills.

'Rwenzororo rebels from Uganda have crossed the mountains to the south,' our informant told us. 'The troops are afraid they're planning to join up with other rebels on this side of the border and are trying to clear them out. Four of the soldiers have been killed so far.' The conversation passed to other topics when a group of commandos came noisily into the bar.

In the 1960s, the Bakonjo tribe, an offshoot of the Zaïrean Banande who lived on the lower slopes of the Ruwenzori Mountains in Uganda, had sought independence from the administrative domination of more powerful tribes and had taken to the hills in guerilla bands, calling themselves 'Rwenzororo'. It was a surprise to find that they were still active. No doubt the recent upheavals in Uganda had given them fresh hope of independence. There would seem to be little prospect of success for them.

Our best chance of transport to Kasindi appeared to be at 5 o'clock next morning when, it was claimed, trucks for the Friday morning market would be leaving Mutwanga. The thought of setting off from Mutsora at 4 am, complete with heavy rucksacks, didn't appeal, but we were saved that ordeal. It turned out that the Conservateur, the head of Mutsora station, was driving to Kasindi next morning and would give us a lift.

We both enjoyed the luxury of a seat in the cab of his pick-up, whilst various members of his staff sat on our rucksacks in the back. This included his driver.

'He's an excellent mechanic, but a drunk. So I prefer to do the driving myself and leave him to tinker with the engine,' the Conservateur explained.

He was one of the new breed of Zaïrean officials, well-educated and efficient. He had only recently returned to Zaïre after completing a master's degree in animal ecology at the University of Göttingen in West Germany. It will be on men like him that the future of Zaïre will depend. At Independence there were very few educated men to run the affairs of the country and, like many other African nations, Zaïre had to rely on the limited resources of the army to provide its leaders. It was encouraging to note that, at last, professional people were starting to gain positions of responsibility. Only time will tell if they will also be allowed the power to address the enormous problems that Zaïre faces.

The presence of the army was very evident as we pulled aside to allow jeeps and lorries to race to the front. Away to our left, the faint pop of gun-fire could be heard along the mountain foothills. We were deposited at the border at the head of a two-mile-long queue of lorries waiting to cross. This is the main road route for transporting the produce of Kivu region out to the East African coast. Kasindi was nothing more than a big village with a larger-than-average market. We were soon through Customs and Immigration with only a modest payment required. There were clearly bigger fish to fry than two backpacking foreigners. The patient queue of trucks no doubt provided richer pickings for officials so inclined.

We had assumed that after passing the Zaïre border post we would immediately enter Uganda. On this assumption we shouldered our packs (we could just carry all our equipment, but not far) and marched off to a new country, only to discover that we had a two-mile trek along the familiar deeply scarred dirt track. The task was not lightened by the sudden onslaught of a tropical storm. Then, as we squelched wearily around yet another bend, the dirt road came to an abrupt end and before us, winding up the hill, was a tarmac dual carriageway complete with road markings and an international traffic sign indicating that vehicles should travel on the left. We were in Uganda. We seemed to have moved forward centuries in the space of a few seconds.

Immigration, customs and police officers were polite and helpful and in no time we were on our way via minibus and pick-up truck to the town of Kasese. The pick-up flew along the potholed tarmac at a speed that terrified us. After so long on dirt roads, we weren't used to high speed travel, especially when lurching about in an open-backed vehicle. Half-way to our destination, the truck slithered to a halt at an army road-block manned by two lads of about 12 or 13 years old, toting automatic weapons. It was with some trepidation that we approached this first meeting with the Ugandan army, but there was no need for concern. With admirable efficiency and reserve, the young soldiers checked the passengers' papers. Handing back our documents, one lad gave a smart salute and with a smile said, 'Welcome to Uganda'. The burden of months of difficult travel through the forests and along the rivers of Zaïre suddenly lifted from our shoulders. We were sure that the going would be easier from now on.

From the Mountains to the Sea

The Queen Elizabeth National Park on the shores of Lake Edward, Uganda, where hippopotami are again establishing themselves after a difficult period.

The Saad Hotel, reputedly the best in Kasese, was full and we were directed to the Moonlight Lodging. Its interior was less romantic than its name suggested, so we opted to return to the Saad for dinner. Over the meal, which bore all the hallmarks of British culinary influence, we met James, the personable young assistant manager.

Our plan up to then had been to spend as little time as possible in Uganda. President Museveni had only recently seized power and the reports we had heard before leaving England were not good.

Large flocks of pelican and other aquatic birds are a particular feature of the National Park.

Even in Kinshasa a British Embassy official had strongly advised us not to go there, but then our experience has been that Embassy staff know little of the country they work in, apart from the capital and its cocktail circuit. More reliable reports from travellers indicated that things were generally quiet, but that there were incidences of armed robbery on the roads. Following Stanley's route, we intended to cross the south-east corner of the country and head for Lake Victoria.

That was the plan, but James persuaded us to spend a couple of days at Mweya Lodge in the Queen Elizabeth National Park, not far from Kasese. He would arrange a taxi for us next day. At least, we thought that was the arrangement. Conversation with James was hard to follow as years of caution over what was said in public had caused him to speak in a habitual low whisper.

We made the right decision. The lodge occupied an outstanding position on a hill overlooking the wide channel that connects Lakes George and Edward (or Lake Ex-Idi Amin as the latter is sometimes known) and the animals that had been slaughtered first for food and later for profit in the bad old days of Idi Amin and Milton Obote were returning to the park in numbers. Our room looked out across the channel to a sandy beach where a herd of elephants came to drink, while hippopotamus heads bobbed up and down in the water nearby. On the hillside behind them, a herd of buffalo grazed peacefully. From the bar on the bougainvillea-covered verandah, more elephants could be seen moving majestically among the candelabra trees and scrub that covered the low, undulating hills of the park. Flocks of white pelicans floated gracefully on the water and, on the lawn just beyond the bar, pintailed whydah

A fish eagle perches high in a tree, spying out the land.

and black-headed weavers busily ignored our presence.

We slept well that night in a real bed with real sheets on a deep soft mattress. Trouble with the pump meant no running water in the bathroom, but a bucket of water was smilingly produced when we asked. A pleasant interlude, but business called. Stanley was never far from our thoughts, and to remind us of our quest was the small town of Katwe and its salt pans which we could see through the haze across Lake Edward. In June 1889 the expedition was marching towards it, expecting trouble.

*****

The occupying forces of Kabba Rega, King of Unyoro, had their headquarters at the village of Katwe at the northern end of the lake. On hearing of Stanley's approach, the commander, Rukara, hurriedly abandoned his position and led his troops into the bush. On 16 June, the expedition entered Katwe unopposed, an event which augured well for the future progress of the caravan. This was a rich area, its wealth based on the salt that was produced and traded far and wide.

Through superior force of arms, Kabba Rega had subjected the salt-gathering tribes to his authority and exacted tribute from them.

Seeing the occupying army fleeing before the expedition's advance, the people welcomed Stanley as a saviour. They were even more delighted to learn that his powerful force had no intention of occupying their land and asked nothing for its services other than friendship and free passage. This the natives gave willingly. For nearly two months the expedition progressed through country, where they were granted rights to take whatever food they required free of charge. This lifted a considerable burden from the shoulders of the leader. The territory through which they were travelling was unexplored, the native reaction to this first European encroachment an unknown factor. Worries over hostile attacks and provision of food evaporated. Stanley's policy of maintaining friendly relations with the local tribes, backed by quiet strength, had paid dividends. Word quickly spreads through the African bush, and the expedition's activities would be known in detail to all the tribes

familiar with the business of harassing passing caravans. The return to 'civilisation' brought with it the endless palavers, the payment of tolls for passage through every petty chief's area and the necessity of buying all the food required to feed the column. Added to this was the inevitable attrition of losing men to relatively well-armed opponents.

Lake Victoria was sighted for the first time on 15 August, and for the next week steady progress was made rounding a large, and unexpected, extension of the lake to the south-west. In 1875 Stanley had circumnavigated Lake Victoria by boat but had missed this part, taking the many islands protecting the bay as the shore line. This was another little geographical discovery to be added to his collection.

*****

Our own jouney to Lake Victoria started at Kasese bus station. Unlike Zaïre, Uganda has a public transport system with a railway and good fast buses on the major routes. We easily found a coach going to Mbarara, paid our money and actually received a ticket in return. This was all very organised. A seat on a bus was much appreciated after the weeks spent on the backs of lorries. Early on the journey, we had to stop at a police control point for papers and passports to be checked. We were still very apprehensive about any contact with armed officials, always expecting trouble and expense. Our fears were quite unfounded here. Greeted by the passengers as friends, the young officers were highly disciplined, polite and efficient. Such a pleasant change from other parts of Africa where a uniform means harassment and extortion.

The road deteriorated as it climbed through vast banana plantations, at the top giving us a view over a wide scrubby plain. Over the next hill and we were looking down on a thickly forested valley, then into an area of tea plantations owned, so a signboard informed us, by the Ankole Tea Company. This was President

The expedition struggles through the precipitous country of Ankori.

ahead of the march long before the column appeared over the horizon.

During July the caravan headed steadily south-east on a line swinging south of Lake Victoria. On 27 July, they crossed the Kagera River, leaving behind what would become the modern state of Uganda and entering the vast plains of Tanzania. Very soon, they also left behind the grateful natives, the free passage and the free food. At a place called Kavari the expedition abruptly re-entered a world

Main street, Mbarara, still to recover from the ravages of the recent civil war.

Museveni's own tribal area and had been at peace for some time, unlike the troubled northern and eastern districts of the country where anti-government rebels were still in operation. It appeared prosperous. The people looked well-fed and well-dressed, many of the women wearing a fashion that must be unique to Uganda, the *basuti*. A long full-skirted dress with big puff sleeves and a square buttoned neck, it is reputed to have originated from a school uniform introduced by a lady missionary at the turn of the century.

The freshly-painted bright blue Mayoba Inn provided a bed for us that night in Mbarara. It was clean and neat. It had electricity, but suffered from what seemed to be a universal problem in Uganda, a lack of running water. An unusual feature was the printed notice on the door:

WARNING

Acts which lead to wetting beds are to be refrained. Please do not use the bed or beddings (the floor or bathroom is recommended).

I think I know what it was getting at!

After a cup of our favourite hot, sweet *chai* in the 'Peaceful Cafe and Bar' next door, we set out to explore the town. There were several large buildings whose functions bore witness to the British influence: a public library, a recreation centre, and even an Inland Revenue office. The picture was completed by a market, several small hotels and restaurants, and some bomb sites which served as reminders of recent troubles. The only other white person we saw was a woman who passed in a Pentecostal Mission vehicle. We were something of a curiosity in the streets of Mbarara, but with a reserve typical of the British, people did not stare and gather round us, laughing, as they would have done in Zaïre. They eyed us discreetly and many wished us 'good afternoon' or 'good evening'. In the popular 'Riheka's Refreshments' restaurant that evening, we were served liver and chips by waitresses in uniform. The colonial heritage was very strong in Uganda, it seemed. The country was such a far cry from Zaïre in so many ways that we felt we had crossed not from one country into another, but from one continent to another.

At the bus station early next morning,

we found the *Kampala Express* ready and waiting with engine running to impress on prospective passengers the immediacy of departure. In fact, it sat idling for a further two hours, while another Kampala-bound bus arrived and left. We were not going all the way to the capital, merely to Masaka, from where another short bus journey would take us to the Uganda–Tanzania frontier. We did not get far that day. We left Mbarara at 9.50 am and at 10.10 am the *Kampala Express* broke down. The driver tried his hand at repairs, then sent the conductor back into town to fetch the bus company's mechanic. On arrival, the latter stripped down the engine to discover that a piston had disintegrated, disappeared back in the direction of Mbarara and returned sometime later with a spare part and an articulate young man who it transpired was the bus company's representative-cum-trouble-shooter. The mechanic soon had the engine back together again. Then all the men tried to push-start the bus: backwards down the hill, up the next hill and then forwards down the hill again. There was a great deal of shouting, cursing and laughing, but only the odd puff of black smoke from the recalcitrant bus. Next an army lorry (requisitioned from a banana company, to judge from the slogan painted on the side) was flagged down and persuaded to tow-start the bus. It was all to no avail. The vehicle seemed beyond hope. The bus crew had shown great tenacity and efficiency, but it was clear that we would be going no further in the *Kampala Express*. The day had slipped away during all this activity and now we had to decide what to do that night. What happened next came as a complete surprise. The trouble-shooter produced a large bag of cash and handed out refunds! True, we only got 90 per cent of the fare paid, but we certainly hadn't expected that. It was 5.30 pm when the soldiers in the banana lorry returned to tell the assembled passengers that it was too dangerous to spend the night on the road, packed us all into their

truck, and in 20 minutes had us back in Mbarara and once again established at the Mayoba Inn.

Our second attempt to leave the town was more successful. A very crowded bus deposited us, after three and a half hours, in Masaka, a big town scenically placed atop a hill with banana plantations rolling away. Shattered buildings testified to the battering it had taken in the recent civil war, although it had clearly been a prosperous town in the past. Even now it was bustling and populous. Food sellers besieged the bus as we pulled in, offering spicy *sambusas*, small solid cakes, bottles of soda, juicy pineapple slices, roast corn cobs and sweets (known as '*shwiti*'). We boarded a smaller bus bound for Mutukula, the border town, and sat waiting for it to depart.

'What do you think of Uganda?' asked a young man in the seat in front.

'Well, we haven't seen very much of it, but we like what we've seen. Everyone is very friendly. And things work here. We've just come from Zaïre, where they often don't.'

The young man seemed pleased.

'We're trying to get back to normal after the bad years,' he said earnestly. 'Ugandans work hard and we think we've got a chance this time.'

We wished him and his compatriots good luck.

Our last bus journey in Uganda took us down a dirt road through a couple of small towns, past groups of isolated huts set in patches of cultivation, big herds of cattle grazing the savannah and finally, close to the border, past an open prison. 'Maybe they hope the prisoners will all escape across the frontier into Tanzania,' suggested John.

Just beyond the prison, a burnt-out armoured car stood abandoned by the roadside, a relic marking the route along which the Tanzanian invasion force crossed into Uganda on its way to topple the Idi Amin regime in 1979.

Mutukula was not what we had expected from a border town. It was a tiny

The Kampala Express *suffering from a terminal illness on the road from Mbarara, Uganda.*

out to be a small room in his friend's backyard. The hole-in-the-ground toilet was one of the more pungent we had come across on our travels.

Getting out of our 'hotel' in the early hours proved more difficult than getting in. The bus to the nearest big town, Bukoba, left from the Tanzanian customs office at 4 am, long before most of Mutukula's residents were awake. Our host had padlocked the high wooden gate that closed off his compound and we couldn't climb over it. We knocked at his door discreetly so as not to waken the rest of the family, but finally had to resort to beating on it and shouting. After what seemed like an eternity, our sleepy, tousled and rather grumpy host emerged and battled with the ancient padlock until it gave way.

There was quite a crowd gathered around the two buses, which consisted of decrepit passenger compartments attached to battered lorry cabs. We sat and waited. Most people dozed. We chatted in a desultory fashion with André, an English accountancy student spending six weeks travelling in East Africa. We had met him over goat stew and *chai* in an eating place the evening before.

At 4.30 am we got off to a push start. We struck a problem almost immediately. The conductor refused to accept our money and we seemed in imminent danger of being thrown off the bus. There had been no exchange facilities at Mutukula and for just such an eventuality John had brought some Tanzanian notes saved from a previous trip. Unbeknown to us, the government had changed the currency in the interim and our notes were no longer legal tender. André luckily had a little of the real stuff and saved the situation by lending us 200 new Tanzanian shillings. We were allowed to continue. Not for long, however. After 18 miles we stopped at Kyaka, the official customs post, where a sleepy man in a white raincoat led us by torchlight into his office to fill out currency declaration

village of just one street with a few shops, a few eating places and a couple of 'hotels'. Customs and immigration formalities were completed relatively quickly and painlessly on both sides of the frontier, but as there was nothing on the Tanzanian side other than the customs house, we were allowed to return to Uganda to spend the night. A young man offered to take us to a hotel. This turned forms. He took a blank piece of paper, wrote out the questions we had to answer then passed it to us to fill in.

'There are no printed forms these days,' he apologised bleakly.

The sun rose in a sky diffused with lemon-yellow hues, then with delicate pinks and blues. Bands of mist lifted slowly from a landscape that was not the Africa we knew. Rocky hillsides and copses of conifers were the dominant features and patches of cultivation rare. The bus picked up dozens of passengers along the route, many of them commuters on their way to work in Bukoba. We were lucky to have a seat. Apart from the overcrowding, the only drawback was the shower of beans that fell on our heads though holes in the roof. Did it rain beans in Tanzania? No, the answer was more prosaic. A sack of beans on the roofrack had a hole in one corner.

Bukoba lies on the western shores of Lake Victoria, the vast inland sea that excited the interest of the nineteenth-century explorers and today divides Tanzania, Uganda and Kenya. For us, the town was a direct link with one of the major players in the Emin Pasha Relief Expedition, Emin Pasha himself. When he returned to the African interior at the head of a German expedition in 1890 his brief was, amongst other things, to establish a settlement on the shores of the Victoria Nyanza. Bukoba was that place.

On our arrival in the morning, my overriding interest was practical rather than historical. It was to find a hotel with running water. Over the last week we had lived out of buckets. One bucket between two doesn't go far when it comes to bathing and washing hair. It certainly doesn't extend to washing clothes. In a town by a lake there seemed to be a good prospect of achieving my ambition. We tried the posh Lake Hotel and the Coffee Tree Inn down by the lake. We tried the Kwabiza Hotel in the town centre. All were full. Finally we found a room at Bukoba's fourth best hotel, the Midland, on a steep rocky hill opposite a big Pentecostal church. The room was clean. There were communal toilets and showers—but no water. So intense was my disappointment that one would have thought a major disaster had occurred, such is the importance that one attaches to these small goals when travelling. However, after another bucket wash, a plate of fried eggs and a restorative cup of *chai*, my flagging spirits were revived and we set off to explore the town.

The market sold colourful vegetables, hunks of meat, creamy-white and brown flour piled up in peaks and mounds of second-hand clothing. There were a large number of shops, mostly, it seemed, run by Indians. The plaques on the buildings showed that many had been built in the 1950s. They bore names such as Jinnah House, Jamal House and Desai Cottage. A huge steel cross crouched on stubby legs over a big Catholic church and small churches and mosques proliferated. We refreshed ourselves with *chai* and *mandazi* (the Tanzanian equivalent of the dough ball) in a tea shop. There were three things we didn't find in Bukoba. The first was beer. The Tanzanians obviously had different priorities from the Zaïreans; whatever else failed in Zaïre, beer supplies always kept going. The second was a toilet roll. Ours had finished and I didn't like to go anywhere without one. The third was any connection with Emin Pasha. There was no statue, no plaque, no street named after him, nothing. Emin Pasha had been swallowed up by Africa. The first two were just items on a very long list of shortages in Tanzania, a reflection of a struggling economic condition; the third a casualty of the country's not unnatural desire to rid itself of its colonial past.

Down by the lake a strong breeze was blowing, and the water was dark blue and choppy. It looked more like a sea than a lake. A herd of goats grazed in the reedy grass by the narrow sandy beach. Beyond, papyrus grew in the lake's marshy rim and beyond that was a rugged green hillside. We walked along the shore

A fishing boat goes about its business on Lake Victoria, near Bukoba, Tanzania.

to the port. Our next move was to cross the lake to Mwanza on the southern shore and from there take a train across Tanzania's vast plains to the Indian Ocean. We bought two second-class tickets, which entitled us to seats on the boat for the following day.

'What time does the boat leave?' John asked.

'Nine o'clock. But be here by 7.30 am,' the ticket clerk advised. 'The big boat's not running at the moment and the small one gets very crowded. With luck you'll be in Mwanza at 5.30 pm.'

In fact it all worked out much better than anticipated. The *Bukoba* was a good-looking ship, bigger than we'd expected, and there were not too many passengers waiting on the dock. First-class passengers had cabins, second-class passengers had wooden seats below deck and third-class had standing room only.

It was a pleasant journey. We played rummy and taught it to an interested onlooker, Onesmo, who then played John and beat him. We met a young German girl working for a Lutheran mission and two managers of a canvas mill, one Tanzanian, the other European.

White-sailed dhows dipped on the blue water as we entered Mwanza Bay. It was 5.30 pm. Perfect timing. We rushed from the boat, keeping ahead of the disem-

barking crowds, to find the smart New Mwanza Hotel. We had no intention of being denied running water this time. Naturally, there was no real need to hurry as there was plenty of room in the hotel. The exorbitant price kept most people away, and we decided we would not be there long ourselves. In the meantime, we revelled in the hot water that really did gush from the shower in our private bathroom. This was our first proper wash since leaving Mambasa in Zaïre 25 days earlier. We were not special enough to warrant one of the only two working air-conditioning units in the hotel. The problem was, as usual, a lack of spare parts. But we were happy enough with the luxury of running hot water.

One or two other things seemed to be in short supply in Mwanza. We found no beer, no Double Cola and no cigarettes in the shops. 'You can only buy cigarettes on the black market,' a shopkeeper furtively informed John. John looked baffled, so the man added helpfully, 'It's down by the Tivoli Cinema'. Sure enough, a row of men standing casually outside the cinema turned out to be black marketeers. One of them approached John.

'Cigarettes? How many do you want?'

'Just one packet,' replied John.

The man looked crestfallen. He hadn't meant how many packets, just how many cigarettes. He only had ten. He called over a friend who had a whole packet and the deal was done. There was no cellophane on the box, but at least the cigarettes inside didn't look too badly mawled.

That evening we discovered where all of Mwanza's beer was. It was disappearing down the throats of the diners and dancers at the disco/video dinner dance in the hotel's Kipepo restaurant. Mwanza's middle class was there in force, dressed in outfits that made us look like a walking jumble sale. Beer was available to diners only and no one knew how long supplies would last. The consequence was that

The dock at Bukoba on Lake Victoria, the town founded by Emin Pasha in 1890.

everyone bought in bottles as if there were no tomorrow. The tables creaked and groaned under the weight and there was certainly no room for food.

'How do they afford it?' I asked Zuberi, the Tanzanian sales manager from the boat. We had baulked at the cost of the dinner dance, but had earlier arranged to meet Zuberi and his colleague, Bill, there and hadn't liked to back out.

'Most of them have got in free. That's why we are having to pay so much,' he answered glumly.

The party was still going strong when we retired at 12.30 am. We weren't used to late nights and loud music any more.

Mwanza was a pleasant town built on the lake shore and on the craggy hills behind Mwanza Bay. It had several bright white mosques and temples, bearing witness to the large Asian presence. In a narrow alley along the wall of the flag-bedecked Sikh temple, a row of fakirs' stalls displayed bottles filled with home-grown medicines. Behind each stall hung a garish illustration of the human body, sectioned off to provide a sort of route map of the ailments that affected the various parts. The bottles, mostly filled with grey or green sludge, also carried illustrations of their curative powers. Next to the fakirs' stalls was the old tin-can section (a tin can, so common in the Western world, is a highly prized item in Africa and has a multiplicity of uses), and beyond that the colourful stalls of the

cotton yarn sellers. There was a carnival atmosphere in the streets on this Muslim holiday Sunday. Throngs of people strolled in the sunshine and gathered down by the lake, where strange rock formations stood a little way out from the shore at crazy angles, topped by cormorants and a fish eagle.

Enquiries at the railway station revealed that all first-class tickets to Dar es Salaam were sold for the next month, so we settled for second class, on the following evening, as far as Tabora, the town half-way across the central plain. We were glad of the opportunity to see Tabora. In the nineteenth century it had been a major Arab settlement on the caravan route into the interior and most European explorers, including Livingstone and Stanley, had stayed there, accepting, incongruously, generous hospitality from men who traded not only in ivory but also in human lives.

Stanley had not visited Mwanza on the expedition that we were following, but his caravan had received a warm welcome just a few miles south at the Church Missionary Society station of Makolo.

*****

On 28 August 1889, the expedition marched into Makolo, to be met by Alexander Mackay, a Scot with a flowing brown beard, dressed in white linen and sporting a grey Tyrolean hat. This was Stanley's first contact with a European representative of the outside world since he had left Yambuya over two years before. It was a significant moment, a return to the known world and a positive sign that the great task was nearing its end. Since leaving Katwe on the northern shore of Lake Edward, the caravan had been gathering speed, covering 440 miles in 47 marches, an average of over 9 miles per day. Now they were just 600 miles from the sea and the end of the torment. But first, the officers and men enjoyed the comfort and order of the mission that brought longed-for relief to their tired bodies and minds. There were books, real coffee, freshly made bread and butter, luxuries which had been no more than a dream for so many months. Their first news from home was consumed with the same eager abandon as the food. Old copies of newspapers and magazines were pored over, every word savoured to the full. Stanley and his officers had for so long existed in a vacuum that this sense of home-coming, even to these reticent and controlled men, must have been a wonderful moment.

The missionary Alexander Mackay had been in Africa for 12 years, of which a considerable number had been spent at the court of the King of Uganda. When the King had turned against Christianity and its growing influence in his kingdom, Mackay had narrowly escaped with his life. Bishop Hannington had been less fortunate, falling victim to the King's desire for retribution, together with scores of native converts. Mackay had fled to the southern end of Lake Victoria to carry on his work from there. It was through him that Emin had managed to get his few dispatches to the coast and he who had helped Dr Junker make his escape. Now he was to be instrumental in easing the expedition's passage to the sea. This would be one of his last acts. By February of the following year he was dead, claimed by a recurring sickness, the plague of all Europeans who ventured into Africa.

Close by was a Catholic mission run by French fathers. This was further good news for the officers as the priests were able to supply them with boots and clothes. All the expedition members were by this time dressed in rags and makeshift garments culled from old blankets. Yet more riches were awaiting them. Some 240 loads had been sent up from the coast by the expedition's organising committee. Now they were fully equipped with trade goods to see them through the last leg of the journey.

The supplies had been delivered by the flamboyant Irish caravan boss, Charles Stokes, who was destined to follow Stanley's route into eastern Congo in 1893, trading guns for ivory and achieving dubious fame as the first European to be executed by the Free State authorities. Stokes's activities highlight a direct consequence of Stanley's trail blazing. The Arabs had originally come to Stanley Falls following the trail pioneered by Stanley in 1877. Again Stanley's route through the Ituri Forest to Lake Albert would pave the way for further Arab expansion. Stokes and others would take advantage of the knowledge gained by Stanley to push west to Lake Edward and on to the Semliki Valley. The Congo Free State, to which Stanley more than any other gave life, turned into a degraded monster once the child was free of his guiding hand. He was without doubt a great explorer, but his efforts did more to spread the scourge of slavery and exploitation of the natives than any other actions of the time. He laboured under the common nineteenth-century hope that he would be followed by missionaries to bring Christianity and 'light' to the darkness and to prepare the way for benevolent trade between the benighted black man and the civilised white. The depressing reality was bondage and destruction for the unfortunate natives.

After 20 days' hospitality at the Makolo mission, the refreshed and re-equipped expedition was ready to start out on the last lap. Many of the expedition followers were less than keen to leave this comfortable billet. On the morning of departure, over 100 people reported too sick to march. A few of the genuine sick were left behind, but the majority had to make the best of it.

*****

Before following Stanley south by train, we experimented with the Tanzanian telephone system in an attempt to book a hotel room in advance in Tabora. We had little confidence that this would be a practical possibility, but, amazingly enough, the phone actually worked, we apparently spoke to the Railway Hotel Tabora and were able to book a room. We were impressed.

We saw a further example of Tanzanian efficiency when we arrived at the railway station at 5 pm, two hours before departure time to allow for problems with our reservation. But there, pinned to the notice board, was a neatly typed seat allocation list and on it were our names. We were in carriage 2205, John in compartment E and I in compartment C. It seemed that mixing of the sexes was not allowed on Tanzanian trains, at least not in second class. People sat, lay and stood around the station building and all the spaces between the bodies were filled with baggage of various shapes and sizes. It was difficult to get through without stepping on some supine figure or its possessions. These were the third-class passengers who had arrived early to be sure of a seat as they did not enjoy the luxury of an allocated position. Suddenly, at a given command, they all leapt to their feet and split into two lines, men to the left and women to the right.

'Do you think the third-class compartments are segregated, too?' I asked John. 'No, I don't think so. I think the idea is to prevent the women and children from being killed in the rush.'

When the two lines had jostled into some sort of order, railway police began to let the passengers through the gates on to the platform, their passage punctuated by frequent cries of 'Fall in!' as some miscreant attempted to barge in out of turn. Was this combination of chivalry and military precision due to an innate Tanzanian sense of fair play or a left-over from colonial times? Whichever it was, it worked a lot better than the systems, or lack thereof, employed at many of the transport termini we had passed through.

We were the first to arrive in our respective second-class compartments (if we had shown more faith in the allocation system, we needn't have turned up so

early). There were six bunks, three on each side. I took the top one on the left as it was less torn and had more foam rubber than the others, some of which were worn down to the bare boards. It looked as though earlier passengers had cut away foam rubber blocks to use as seat cushions at home. Gradually, the compartments filled up. At first there were seven adults and a child in my ladies-only compartment, but the extraneous number seven soon left. John's compartment also had an extra body, but this one argued his case and refused to leave until the ticket inspector came around at 1 o'clock in the morning and threw him out.

At 7.15 pm the engine gave a mournful hoot, the last passengers, who were buying roast corn cobs and cakes from stalls on the platform, scuttled aboard, and we pulled slowly out of Mwanza Station. John and I stood in the corridor, where it was cooler and less claustrophobic. My ladies obviously didn't believe in letting in night air and kept the window tightly shut all the way.

Rugged hillsides stood silhouetted against a pale evening sky and the lake gleamed silver. The rocky outcrops soon gave way to a plain dotted with bushes and small trees, some resembling old-fashioned telegraph posts with spiky top knots. The moon was full. Its brilliance blanched the landscape to an eerie lunar desert, at one point interrupted by the orange glow of a necklace of bush-fires.

At 8 pm, the clanging of a gong announced dinner. We climbed over the squatting figures gathered at the end of the carriage by the toilet, presumably refugees from third class, took our life in our hands as we stepped across the gap between the footplates, and continued down the train until we reached the restaurant car. We ate hearty platefuls of unidentifiable meat and potatoes and, to our surprise, were offered bottles of Safari lager. It seemed that the Tanzania Tourist Corporation, who ran the New Mwanza

Hotel, and Tanzania Railways had a monopoly over beer distribution.

Back outside compartment C, I had a conversation in rudimentary Swahili with one of my fellow inmates. Unfortunately, the Swahili I had learnt from an elderly little book entitled *Upcountry Swahili*, whose author had assured me in his introduction that the pure form of the language was spoken only on the coast, proved to be 30 years out of date and from the wrong country. My mentor had learnt his upcountry Swahili in Kenya. However, I raised quite a few laughs, which is never a bad thing.

Once we were all inside the compartment, the ladies firmly bolted the door and piled a few heavy sacks against it for good measure. I was not sure whether they were guarding against theft or against attacks on their virtue. They were puritanical in their modesty, considering it was a girls-only dormitory. I was the only one who took any clothes off, wriggling out of boots, socks and trousers after lights out in the small space between the bunk and the ceiling. I had unrolled my sleeping bag and, despite the heat, fell sound asleep, rocked by the soothing motion of the train. We were all rudely awakened by a banging on the door at 1 o'clock in the morning. It was, announced a voice, the ticket inspector. Well, the girls weren't going to fall for that one. One of them held the bolt firmly in place, while another dragged a heavy bundle to join the large pile already defending the door. After five minutes of knocking, cajoling, pleading, threatening and shouting, the ticket inspector admitted defeat and moved on. We all went back to sleep, pure and unmolested.

I was awakened once again at 6 am when the train came to a halt. It couldn't be Tabora. We weren't due to arrive there until 7 am. But indeed it was Tabora, the girls assured me. A train arriving an hour early? It was unheard of. On the platform outside I could hear a great number of voices, one close to the window shouting, 'Julie, wake up.

We're here!' It was John, who had managed to fight his way off the train through the mass of people thronging the corridor. I prised open the window, pushed out my rucksack, then remembered to pull on my trousers. No time to lace up my boots. I emerged on to the platform two minutes later, my sleeping bag clutched in my arms. My hair was tousled and I kept tripping over my bootlaces. It was not a very dignified entry into Tabora.

The Tabora Railway Hotel was delightful, an old German colonial building, white with a red roof and flowering bougainvillea trailing over the wide entrance. The only trouble was, at 6.15 in the morning there was no one except the nightwatchman and ourselves there. We sat in deep wooden armchairs on the open verandah and waited, as darkness dispersed and the sun slowly rose. We finally checked in and found our room, one of the small cheap ones at the end of the corridor. I made straight for the washbasin. Yes, there was running water. And the toilet two doors down flushed. I may be thought to have a fixation about water, but it is taken so much for granted in the developed world and is such a luxury everywhere else.

Breakfast was an uplifting experience. The dining room was a baronial hall, 40 feet high, with wooden panelling and a chandelier. We felt a little overawed eating bread and jam in such a room. We were joined at breakfast by Siegfried, a German employed on a telephone installation project at stations between Tabora and the two railheads of Mwanza and Kigoma. He spoke little English and we spoke no German, but Siegfried didn't let that hinder him and we chatted away, to mutual happy confusion, until he had to leave for work. We next tackled the hotel manager as we had a booking for only one night and had been told that the place was full. He tacitly accepted that possession is nine points of the law and agreed to let us keep our room for a second night. We had yet to establish how long

The old steam shed at Tabora, the graveyard for dozens of locomotives dating from the days of the East African Railway system.

we would have to stay in Tabora. This would depend on the availability of space on the train.

Down at the station, we soon discovered that all berths on the next train to Dar es Salaam in two days' time—and for weeks to come—were reserved. When it was obvious that we had no intention of going away empty-handed, the ticket clerk suggested we speak to the station master. This was clearly positive discrimination—in favour of whites—but comfort came before scruples and we followed up his suggestion. The station master, Mathias Kajogoo, was charming and helpful. He looked at his schedule and pointed to a first-class berth reserved in the name of Krug.

'Mr and Mrs Krug made their reservation some weeks ago, but I have a feeling they've decided to fly instead of going by train.'

'Yes, I think you're right,' I chimed in.

'We heard this morning they're taking the plane.'

During our conversation with Siegfried, a German couple, a plane and Dar es Salaam had been mentioned. Actually, it turned out that I had misunderstood and he was not talking about the Krugs at all. Fortunately, as the station master then proceeded to allocate their berths to us, the Krugs didn't materialise at the station on departure day and I was saved the embarrassment of having to explain why we appeared to be sharing their first-class compartment.

At the station master's suggestion, we went to see the Chief Engineer, Dr Kailembo, in the afternoon to arrange a tour of the marshalling yards. We found that he lived at the Railway Hotel, too. He was a youngish man and had trained in the Soviet Union. He had returned home with a pretty, blonde Russian wife and a small child called Sasha. The

143

marshalling yards were a railway buff's dream. There were modern Canadian Type 88 and German Type 64 locos and over 50 old steam engines, left-overs from the days of the East African Railways, which sat rusting in the steam shed or out on disused track. Two of them still worked and were used for shunting. It was a marvellous sight to see these two old war horses chugging powerfully along with a full head of steam. Unfortunately, it seemed they were to be phased out over the next two or three years.

'Tabora's a busy junction,' Richard Kailembo told us. 'We have a minimum of 15 trains a day, mostly freight, going through. From here to Dar can be a problem with heavy wagons. The gradient's very steep in places and the engines can't always hold them. You'll see quite a bit of junk by the line as you go.'

Next morning we set out to track down the Livingstone Memorial Museum at Kwihara, about six miles away. Our taxi driver and his mate, who came along to push or carry out on-the-spot repairs, had never visited the museum and seemed to feel they were setting out on a wild goose chase. But they found it easily enough, driving along dirt roads through a dry, still landscape dotted with skinny trees and bush. The museum, built in 1957, was a replica of the Arab *tembe* (guest house) in which first the explorers, Burton and Speke, and later Stanley and Livingstone, had stayed during their travels. The place was known to them then as Kazeh. The museum keeper, roused from a mid-morning nap in his house behind the *tembe*, produced a large key and opened the big carved doors that led into the building from the shady verandah. The walls were built of mud bricks, a couple of feet thick, with square window holes and the roof was solidly thatched. The rooms, cool and free of insects, were set around a square courtyard where pomegranate trees used to grow and where donkeys had been tethered at night. They consisted of a living room, bedrooms, kitchen, bathrooms and servants' quarters.

It must have been a very pleasant and comfortable existence.

In one of the rooms was a collection of cuttings about the Stanley–Livingstone expedition from the *New York Herald*, the newspaper whose publisher, Gordon Bennett, had commissioned Stanley to find the famous missionary–explorer. There were also photostats of Livingstone's maps and letters.

The carved and studded 'Arab' door of the re-constructed tembe *at Kwihara, near Tabora. Many European explorers spent time here, most notably Stanley and Livingstone in 1872.*

Next to the tembe *at Kwihara, a cross marks the last resting place of John William Shaw, who accompanied Stanley on his expedition in search of Livingstone.*

From the verandah we looked, as Stanley and Livingstone must have done before us, over a dry, but pleasant vista of mango trees and low hills. Outside stood the very mango tree under which the two men had said goodbye in 1872 after spending six months together at Kazeh. They had come to this spot, after their first meeting at Ujiji on Lake Tanganyika, to give the doctor a chance to recuperate from illness and to re-equip for his last venture into the heart of Africa. Fifty yards beyond the *tembe* was the grave of William Shaw, who had died whilst accompanying Stanley on the search for Livingstone. On his departure, Stanley returned to Europe to instant fame, and to embark on a new career as an explorer in his own right. This was our first positive contact, the first record of the existence of Stanley in Africa that we had found in all our travels. It was encouraging to know that his elusive ghost had some substance at last.

Next morning we were up at 5.30 am as the train was scheduled to leave at 6.45 am. At the station we found the train from Kigoma was in, but not the one from Mwanza. The two were to join together at Tabora to form the big Dar train. We were a bit concerned that no allocation list was posted up, as it had been at Mwanza, but our friend the station master assured us we had been allocated compartment D of the first-class carriage on the train standing in the station. As usual, we were the first to arrive. The other passengers obviously knew that nothing would happen for a couple of hours. The Mwanza train arrived at 9 am and, after some shunting, we finally set off on the 520-mile journey to Dar es Salaam. If all went according to plan, we should be in the capital by mid-morning the following day, a rate of travel that, a hundred years earlier, was unthought of. The route that we would travel in a matter of a few days had taken the Stanley expedition more than three months' labour.

* * * * *

September and the first half of October had passed uneventfully, with the caravan settling into a routine of steady progress. On 17 October it arrived at the staging post of Ikungu, on the main east–west caravan route between the coast, Tabora and Ujiji on Lake Tanganyika. It seemed a busy spot to Stanley and his officers. First, two Catholic fathers, Girault and Schintze from the mission on Lake Victoria, caught them up and joined the party for the remainder of the trip. Then an Arab caravan arrived on its way to Lake Tanganyika with goods for Tippu Tip.

Having joined the main road across Africa, Stanley's primary problem was to try to keep within reasonable bounds the escalating demands for '*honga*' (toll payment) of every petty chief along the route. There was a particularly trying region called Ugogo that might have been more aptly named 'Ustaystay'. If all the demands made on the caravan there had been met, there would have been no resources left with which to continue. This area Stanley described as 'a ferment of

trouble and distraction'. He concluded that the chiefs must have gone through some special training to be so objectionable: 'One would think that there was a school somewhere in Ugogo to teach low cunning and vicious malice to the chiefs, who are masters in foxy-craft.'

It was 10 November, and just 200 miles from the coast, when the expedition made its first contact with the Germans on entering a fort at Mpwapwa. They were warmly welcomed by the garrison commander, Lieutenant Rochus Schmidt, who insisted on providing Stanley with an escort to the coast as an excuse to abandon his remote and boring posting. They spent three days at the post and, thanks to a local English missionary, had another opportunity to indulge in news from home, scanning a year's back issues of the *Weekly Times*. This was another step in preparing themselves to meet the

different world at the coast. At least they would have some cocktail conversation and not feel completely the country cousins.

They marched on. Now that they were moving through areas under German control, all sorts of luxuries were pressed on the officers to ease the rigours of camp life. Letters started to arrive, the first they had received since the early days on the Congo. In late November, the expedition was camped at Msua, less than 50 miles from the sea, when the outside world broke into their closed society in the form of two reporters. Showing a little of Stanley's early journalistic flair, the two Americans, Thomas Stevens and Edmund Vizetelly, had put together a caravan and raced out to be first with the exclusive story of the expedition. This was just the sort of scoop for which Stanley had been famous. Vizetelly had the

The appearance of two American reporters at Msua camp is cause for a celebration.

146

inside track for the story as he represented the *New York Herald*, Stanley's old paper, and came loaded down with presents and congratulations from his former employer and sponsor of two expeditions, James Gordon Bennett. Stanley was well prepared for the occasion, the articles already written and available to the highest bidder. The next morning, it was the *New York Herald*'s runners who were racing to the coast to bring the story to the world. Stanley's transition from leader of a doomed and struggling expedition to the hero of the hour was almost complete.

On the evening of 3 December, whilst sitting around the camp fire, they heard a dull boom in the far distance. There was a moment's silence then, as realisation dawned, a great cheer went up from the hundreds of voices in the camp. The sound they had heard was the evening gun fired from Zanzibar. This was their last night on the road. Tomorrow they would reach Bagamoyo and see again the rolling surf of the Indian Ocean.

The next day, the expedition was met by the commander of Bagamoyo, Major Wissman, a man who had served under Stanley in the Congo. Horses were brought up, Stanley and Emin Pasha mounted, and leaving the officers to bring in the caravan, rode into the palm-decked streets to acknowledge the cheers of the crowds and accept their welcome as conquering heros. The 50-year-old white-haired figure, racked with sickness and bent under the weight of so much responsibility, straightened his back, lifted his cap and smiled. The transition was complete, Stanley had returned triumphant to the world stage.

*****

Our arrival at the coast was somewhat less triumphal. On leaving Tabora, the train travelled through areas of grass and scrub, strewn with mango trees, a reminder of all the Africans who had marched into slavery across these plains, scattering in their path stones from the mango fruits that were often all they had to eat. The scrub gave way to sparse dry woodland interspersed with low-growing fan palms. We stopped at occasional small villages whose only link with the outside world appeared to be the railway. At Goweleo, villagers ran up and down the track offering pawpaws, bananas, *mandazi* (dough balls), corn cobs, cooked sweet potatoes and a sugary drink called *halia* to the passengers leaning out of the windows.

The tall woodland was replaced by thick dry bush as we approached Itigi. This was a small town rather than a village and the first place where a road had met the railway line since Tabora. From a close study of our maps, it also seemed that we were just a few miles south of the old caravan route, and the point where Stanley joined the main east–west track at Ikungu. Names we found a problem when trying to follow the explorers' routes. What they wrote down was what they thought they heard, a system that often led to confusion. Ikungu has disapeared from the maps, but Issuna seemed to be in the right place. Anyway, we were happy to think that we were back on the trail of the elusive explorer. This put us in the region of Stanley's 'Ugogo', where the chiefs' business acumen had caused such trouble and expense. The Wagogo were still keen traders. With the loss of the caravan traffic they had turned their attention to the modern equivalent, the train. The station was packed with traders engaged in high speed deals with the passengers. Added to the usual selection of fruit and vegetables was a range of hand-made items: wooden combs and spoons, animal carvings, woven baskets and brushes.

Beyond Itigi, herds of hump-backed cattle grazed on the seemingly barren plain between small plantations of cotton and maize. At Manyoni, disaster struck when the *chai* stall on the station ran out of our favourite hot sweet tea just as John reached the front of the queue, plastic cups held before him in useless supplication. After Manyoni, the land became

more hilly with outcrops of rock and flat-topped acacias, then began the descent from the plain. Richard Kailembo's 'junk', twisted and derailed wagons, littered the track side. Saranda lay at the end of the descent, a pretty station bedecked with bougainvillea and frangipani, spruced-up and ready for inspection in any best-kept-station competition. Huge baobabs were now scattered among thick bush. Along the track, tribesmen wearing dark cloths around thin bodies leant on spears and watched our passage. Around them lay the railway 'junk', a strange juxtaposition of ancient and modern.

By 6.15 pm, we were 192 miles from Tabora, at a place called Kintinku, having averaged about 25 miles an hour. This was by no means the fastest train in the world. A group of baboons, gathered round a candelabra tree near the line, busily ignored the passing train. Animal tracks traced patterns across the dusty landscape, but the animals themselves kept out of sight. As the sun set, a troupe of monkeys leapt through the trees silhouetted against the vivid evening sky.

It was dark when we pulled into Dodoma, the geographical heart of Tanzania and the country's proposed new capital. Already parliament met from time to time in the small town, putting unbearable pressure on its limited infrastructure. Situated some 280 miles from Dar es Salaam, with communications a major problem, the idea of turning Dodoma

At each stop made by the train to Dar es Salaam, traders carried on a brisk business with the passengers. By the track, heaps of 'junk' bore witness to the dangers of overloading wagons on steep descents.

into a viable capital city seemed doomed to failure. The one thing in its favour—the production of a quite palatable 'Dodoma' wine—is hardly the major requirement of a city at the hub of the country's administration. Plump purple grapes and kebabs were the specialities on offer on Dodoma Station.

We slept soundly as the train trundled on through the night, awakening to find the countryside less dry and dusty. A quick look at the map indicated that we must have passed through the Nguru Mountains in the early hours and were now only about 75 miles from the sea. Large villages had sprung up along the line, plantations of bananas, potatoes, manioc and pineapples fanning out around them.

As we approached the capital, we passed into an area of hills and thickly-wooded valleys where palm trees grew in abundance. The outskirts of the city resembled a continuous village of mud and thatch huts surrounded by *shambas* (fields), which gave way to small houses built of permanent materials. Further in, suburbs proliferated to one side of the line, an industrial area occupied the other. The train made its way slowly through the city, crossing wide roads with their long lines of waiting traffic, then passed a complex of marshalling yards packed with broken and rusting rolling stock, and suddenly we were there. A nondescript station to struggle along with our luggage, everyone busy about their own affairs, our only welcome the insistent entreaties of taxi drivers. We had crossed Africa, but that was a private pleasure to be savoured alone as we were swallowed up in the bustle and noise of the big city.

Journey's End

Dar es Salaam marked our arrival at the coast, but not the end of our quest. To follow the story of the Emin Pasha Relief Expedition to its conclusion, we still had two more places to visit, Bagamoyo and the island of Zanzibar. Bagamoyo is just 43 miles north of the capital along the coast, but it entailed a return to road travel. We had established the fact that buses regularly made the journey. Now all we had to do was find one. This was easier said than done. Dar es Salaam is a large, confusing city and we seemed to have been walking for hours by the time we found the dusty little back street, near the market, where the buses started from. We climbed into a bus destined for Bagamoyo and sat and waited for an hour. At first it was crowded, but slowly people drifted away until we were the only ones left. Getting out to investigate, we discovered two wheels had been removed. We took a taxi instead.

Bagamoyo is today a sleepy backwater displaying little evidence of its past importance. We went first to a small museum about a mile beyond the town at the impressive Catholic mission, which represents the only attempt that has been made to record the town's history. The exhibition told the story of the slave trade for which the town was the main east coast transit point. For those slaves who survived the long trek across Africa, this was their last view of their homeland. Indeed, tradition has it that the very name Bagamoyo means 'Here I lay down my heart'. It was surprising to learn that the slave trade did not end in this part of the world until the 1920s. However, it was not the slave trade that concerned us at present, but the town as it was during German colonial times. We had come to search out one particular building which had played a part in the Emin Pasha saga and which we hoped still existed. It was the original German headquarters and officers' mess.

Walking down a sandy track to the beach, we passed the crumbling fortifications of the old customs house. At the water's edge, an orderly queue of people waited to board a boat for the trip across to Zanzibar. A little further along the beach, a shipyard was well advanced with its latest contract, a wooden sailing dhow, a craft that is still active in the coastal waters. Standing back from the shore was the imposing bulk of the German 'Boma' (fort) around whose semi-circular wall large metal plaques served as memorials to soldiers who had died in the Bushiri uprising at the turn of the century. Another plaque, its wording now almost obliterated, commemorated the start of Burton and Speke's expedition of 1857. But there was no mention of Stanley, even though two of his expeditions had set out from this spot, and one had ended nearby in dramatic circumstances. The *boma* was not built until 1897 and was not what we were looking for. That building we found a hundred yards or so further on. The old headquarters and mess was a two-storey Arab house, streaked with grime and flaking plaster, an open staircase at the side leading to the first floor. It was in that upper room that the return of Stanley and Emin to the coast was celebrated on the evening of 4 December 1889.

*****

The reception the expedition received was all they could have wished for. The banquet was a sumptuous affair, the food magnificent and the celebration carried forward in 'a flood of champagne'. Thirty-four people sat down to dinner to honour the safe return of H M Stanley and Emin Pasha. Consuls and captains had come

from Zanzibar, a German naval band played in the corner of the room, and the host, Major Wissman, provided the best of everything for his guests. It was a heady experience for men who had struggled for three years to cross Africa and been reduced to scavenging for insects and fungi to stay alive.

The after-dinner speeches were given by Wissman, Stanley and Emin. There was no word of discord to be heard, just gratitude for their deliverance and arrival in this haven of plenty. The speeches over, the room filled once more with the sounds of convivial conversation and the band played on. Below, in the courtyard, a more boisterous party was in full swing as the expedition porters celebrated in their own way with music, song and dance. Emin moved from table to table, talking in German and English, obviously enjoying himself, his mood 'supremely gay and happy'.

Stanley was deep in conversation with Major Wissman, discussing the political aspirations of the Germans in East Africa, when his servant hurried up to him and whispered in his ear. Evidently not understanding the message, he was heard to say, 'What, fallen over a chair?'
'No, the verandah, sir', was the response from the wide-eyed servant. Stanley pushed back his chair and walked briskly from the room. It was only then that it was noticed that the guest of honour, Emin Pasha, was missing. Others rushed after Stanley to see what had happened. Outside the only evidence was a pool of blood on the ground. The Pasha had already been taken to the hospital, where he lay unconscious with a suspected fractured skull. Wandering short-sightedly out on to the balcony, he had managed to fall over the edge and crash to the ground below. This was the bizarre end to Stanley's last, troubled African expedition.

Before continuing the triumphal progress in a flotilla of naval vessels to Zanzibar on 6 December, Stanley paid what was to be his last visit to Emin Pasha. The patient had recovered consciousness

and was well enough to assure Stanley that he was not about to die. After an attempt to have the Pasha moved to Zanzibar was blocked on medical grounds, Stanley had no option but to abandon his one tangible prize from three years' work and leave Emin in the hands of his fellow countrymen. Stanley was to have no further direct contact with the ex-governor of Equatoria province.

On arrival in Zanzibar, the affairs of the expedition were finalised. The surviving Zanzibaris were paid off and the widows and orphans of the 400 men who

Emin's fall cracks his skull and forces him to remain in Africa; Stanley is robbed of his prize.

The expedition's last camp at Bagamoyo.

did not return received compensation. The contingent of 290 refugees from Equatoria, less 30 of Emin's personal staff who had remained with him, caused so much trouble on the island with their drunken and riotous behaviour that they had to be moved to less tempting quarters at Mombasa to await their return to Egypt. Between seeing to these matters, attending banquets and dealing with the flood of congratulatory telegrams, Stanley found time to reap his revenge on Tippu Tip.

The Arab caravans that plied their trade from Zanzibar were sponsored by Indian financiers who provided the trade goods, took a hefty slice of the profits when the caravans returned, and also acted as bankers for the Arabs. Tippu Tip's banker was a man named Taria Topan. From him, Stanley learnt that he was holding £10,600 of Tippu's money, paid by the Congo Free State for ivory

traded out of Stanley Falls. A quick calculation was made of the losses caused to the expedition, in Stanley's opinion, by Tippu Tip's failure to honour his agreement to supply men to the Rear Column. To no one's surprise, this figure came to £10,000. An injunction was taken out to prevent the Arab trader gaining access to this money before he had presented himself at Zanzibar to answer Stanley's charges. This action of Stanley's was to prove a source of embarrassment to Sir William Mackinnon and his associates, who had more important business to transact with the Sultan of Zanzibar. In due time, all charges against Tippu were dropped, but not before they had caused him a great deal of trouble and inconvenience. He felt obliged to leave his post in the middle of Africa and make the long journey to Zanzibar, where, on his eventual arrival, he found that there was no charge to answer. With Tippu away,

things soon went badly for the Arabs in the eastern Congo. Fighting started, firstly amongst themselves, then with the Free State authorities, who took advantage of the situation to wrest control from the Arabs and drive them out. Tippu Tip's Central African empire was lost, and with it most of his wealth. In the end, he paid a high price for getting on the wrong side of H M Stanley.

The expedition's third Christmas together was spent in the more congenial surroundings of Zanzibar, where final preparations for departure were being made. Jephson was sent over to Bagamoyo to make one last attempt to persuade Emin to accompany the officers to Cairo, but to no avail. He still felt his place was with 'his people'. The only thing that seemed to have changed was that 'his people' were no longer the ragamuffins of Equatoria, but his compatriots, the

A naval escort takes Stanley and his men to Zanzibar.
ABOVE

The reception party awaits Stanley's arrival at the British Consulate at Zanzibar Town.
BELOW

Jephson, Nelson, Stanley, Parke, Stairs and the surviving porters pose for a last picture at Zanzibar.

Germans. He had re-discovered his national identity. After years of masquerading as a Turk, Eduard Schnitzer, alias Emin Pasha, was again proud to be a German. Jephson's visit was the last contact that any member of the Relief Expedition was to have with Emin Pasha.

*****

Out of a misplaced sense of adventure and a quest for authenticity, we chose to sail to Zanzibar in a small fishing boat, along with 50 others. The MV *Maymoun* was a wooden-hulled vessel with central engine house. A covered area at the stern contained a cooking fire, while the rest of the deck, topped by a tall wooden hoist, was open. At first, the voyage was enjoyable, but once away from the coast, the sea became choppy and most of the passengers turned green. John, unusually for him, was seasick and I only survived by adopting a horizontal position on the cargo hold with my hat over my face as protection from the sun. This torture lasted

seven hours, before the beautiful sweep of bay before Zanzibar Town came into sight, the white buildings perched above coral sands lapped by a blue-green sea. White-sailed dhows swooped around us like dolphins, guiding us towards the sanctuary of the dhow harbour and terra firma.

We stayed at the Zanzibar Hotel, an old Arab house with beamed ceilings, a great carved and studded door and in its hallway an ancient brass inlaid Arab chest. The hotel was in the old quarter of Zanzibar Town, known as Stone Town, a maze of narrow streets and passages lined with tall white houses and open-fronted shops, most with intricately carved wooden doors complete with big brass locks and studwork. Overhanging the alleyways were enclosed lattice-work balconies, where ladies used to take the air, unseen, as custom required. In the faces of the people who strolled the streets or sat chatting in doorways we could see the elements that make up the history of the

The MV Maymoun *provided a colourful, but uncomfortable, way of travelling between Dar es Salaam and Zanzibar.*

STANLEY: "Well, Emin, old fellow, this cup of the United Kingdom Tea Company's Delicious Tea makes us forget all our troubles."
EMIN: "So it does, my boy."

UNITED KINGDOM TEA COMPANY, LIMITED.

Offices: 21, Mincing-lane, London.   Duty-paid Stores: Imperial Warehouse, Leman-street, London.

The tea advertiser's idea of the idealised relationship between Emin and Stanley was far from the truth.

The water front of Zanzibar Town. In Stanley's time this would have been a bustling place with the bay full of shipping.

island: Bantu, Arab, Swahili, Shirazi (settlers from the Persian Gulf), Asian and European.

Still diligently in pursuit of Stanley, we had applied for access to the National Archives, to search for evidence there of the expedition that seemed to have been erased without trace from the rest of Africa. We had to wait a few days for permission, so we took advantage of the delay to look at what Zanzibar had to offer. Our guide was a colourful local character called Mr Mitu, who took us around town in his ancient taxi. The house that had once been home to Tippu Tip was a dark, mouldering building badly in need of a coat of paint, and the wall plaque that marked the old British Consulate, where Stanley had often been entertained, now sat in the middle of a large brightly painted mural advertising soap powder. In better condition was the house known as Livingstone's House, half a mile from

Stone Town, where the missionary–explorer had stayed on several occasions. A cool, pleasant building overlooking the sea, it was now the offices of the Friendship Tourist Bureau, but contained few reminders of Livingstone himself. On the shore road, overlooking the bay and harbour, stood the beautifully restored *Beit-el-Ajeib*, the 'House of Wonder', once the Sultan's palace and now the offices of the single political party, the *Chama Cha Mapinduzi* (Party of the Revolution). A gleaming white three-story building, it had a tall clock tower and wide lattice-work verandahs around its three floors.

On the site of the old slave market stood the Cathedral Church of Christ, a Gothic heap built by Edward Steere, first Bishop of Zanzibar, between 1873 and 1880. The altar was erected on the very spot where a slave whipping post used to stand. On a wall hung a crucifix, reputed

157

Sailing dhows are still used to trade up and down the East African coast and smaller versions, like this one in the bay off Zanzibar Town, are used for fishing. ABOVE LEFT

Zanzibar is a haven of deserted bays and white sand beaches. ABOVE RIGHT

The Sultan's House of Wonder was completed in the 1880s. The 'wonder' was that it was the first building on Zanzibar to be equipped with electric light. BELOW LEFT

to be made from the wood of the tree under which Livingstone's heart was buried. Wood from this tree was as popular a talisman as splinters from the 'true' cross. It must have been a very large tree!

Moving out into the countryside, our enthusiastic guide, Mitu, demonstrated the natural riches of Zanzibar, hitching up his striped robe and shinning up trees to fetch us an abundance of fruits, spices and nuts: cloves, cinnamon, soursops, mangosteens, lychees, oranges, pomelos, tangerines, limes, lemons, starfruit, custard apples, durians, breadfruit, jack

Our guide to Zanzibar, Mr Mitu, displays the day's haul of the island's riches in fruit and spices. BELOW RIGHT

fruit, coconuts, coffee beans and cocoa pods. The list seemed endless. Many of these fruits had originally come from the Indonesian spice islands, but now the trade was moving in the opposite direction. The main buyers of Zanzibar's clove crop are the Indonesians, who use the clove as an ingredient in their cigarettes.

After driving back through the lush green countryside, past small villages served by a network of picturesque old wooden buses, it was quite a shock on entering Zanzibar Town to see the serried ranks of the Michanzani workers' flats, horrendous modern dwellings built by the East Germans in their drabbest style for the revolutionary government. Their one saving grace was that the accommodation, we were told, was rent-free. From an aesthetic point of view, it was a relief to escape back to the homely neglect of Stone Town. Zanzibar's museum actually held one or two artifacts and

mementoes from Stanley's expeditions. Our request for a closer look at these items was thwarted as no one could find the keys to the cabinets. The staff were, in any case, much more interested in earning a few shillings by hiring out the venerable giant tortoises in the gardens for visitors to sit on to be photographed, and could not understand our refusal to take part in what we considered a cruel use of the animals.

At last, permission came through for our visit to the National Archives. We hired bicycles and, like good students, cycled the couple of miles down the airport road to a low modern building. Seated in a study area on the first floor, we were presented with a bundle of green manila folders. Leafing through the documents, we found the Zanzibar element of the Emin Pasha Relief Expedition story. In our hands we held seemingly unexciting records of payments to porters and legal documents detailing Stanley's dispute with Tippu Tip. But we were happy. Many of the documents were in Stanley's own hand and we felt that we had at last made contact with the elusive ghost that we had been seeking for so long.

The SS Katoria *carries Stanley to Egypt.*

The SS Katoria *carries Stanley to Egypt.*

For 90 days we had followed the shadowy figure of Stanley across the breadth of Africa and had, in the end, found these few scraps of paper to provide the slenderest of links with a moment in history. Stanley lives on in his writings and in the memory of his deeds, but in the great forests, along the rivers, in the mountains and across the plains, his passing has been swallowed up by the vastness of Africa. And that, perhaps, is as it should be. The reality of Africa is of the moment not of the past. Like a paddle slicing through the waters of a great river, the expedition was just a ripple in the passage of time, soon to be consumed by the relentless flow of events. On our journey we had hardly scratched the surface. We had made no mark on Africa, but Africa, as it had for Stanley and all those who travelled there, had made a mark on us.

*****

On 16 January 1890, Stanley and his men arrived in Cairo, delivered 260 refugees from Equatoria into the hands of the Egyptian government, and there, finally, ended the Emin Pasha Relief Expedition. What had been achieved? None of the main objectives had been realised. In spite of sacrificing the lives of two Europeans and hundreds of Zanzibari and native carriers, they had failed to deliver substantial 'relief' to the province of Equatoria. Their ignorance of the true situation in the province had rendered the immediate plans of King Leopold and Sir William Mackinnon obsolete. Certainly, a number of refugees had been returned to their government, but a government that had thought itself well rid of them. The one great prize, the province's governor, had been successfully removed to the coast, but there, through cruel and uncompromising fate, had been snatched away. Certainly, the sum of geographical knowledge had been supplemented by the expedition's discoveries, but, above all, this crossing of Africa had been a massive human achievement. It is difficult to believe that any would have returned to tell the tale without the outstanding leadership of the greatest African explorer of the nineteenth century, Henry Morton Stanley.

The last word on Emin Pasha comes from William Hoffman, Stanley's servant, writing many years after the event and reflecting the view of all the officers who accompanied him across Africa:

He was a strange, inexplicable man, this Governor of the Equatoria Province. Some people have ranked him with Gordon as one of the world's heroes. But those, like myself, who knew him and journeyed across Africa in his company, have a very different tale to tell, a tale of vacillations which he called loyalty, of ingratitude to the man who risked his own life to go to his rescue, of selfishness and indecision and childish temper. In my opinion, at last, he was not worthy of the lives, white and black, that were laid down in his cause. He was not worthy to be rescued.

Epilogue

The story of Emin Pasha and Equatoria did not end with the expedition. There was many a twist still to come. Casting aside the more lucrative offers he received, Emin, on his recovery, chose to stay in Africa and take employment with the Germans. On 26 April 1890 he led an expedition back to the African interior, his task to show the German flag and to establish a presence on Lake Victoria and in the wild and ill-defined areas bordering the Congo Free State. The Germans, like Stanley, were soon to discover that their new convert was more trouble than he was worth.

From the outset, his primary interest was in his natural history studies. Back at the coast, his employers were exasperated to receive tons of specimens, but few reports on his political and military tasks. His one solid achievement was the founding of the town of Bukoba on the south-western shore of Lake Victoria. But he soon tired of this work and the pull of Equatoria seemed too strong to resist. With a small caravan, he embarked on the crazy project of finding a route across the continent to the Cameroons, his idea being to link the two German possessions in East and West Africa. This took him out of the Germans' sphere of influence and was entirely against orders. In April 1891, he received instructions to return to the coast, but he ignored these and pressed on.

Retracing the route he had taken with Stanley, he came to the southern end of Lake Albert, to find that one of his former officers, Selim Bey, was camped there with a small band of followers. Equatoria province was now split into three areas: along the Nile, to the north, the forces of the Mahdi held sway; at the northern end of the Lake a rebel leader, Fadl el Mulla, was stationed with most of the troops who had remained behind; and Selim with his small band held the south. It transpired that Selim had followed Stanley, found the ammunition that he had buried and had settled down amongst the friendly natives, only for Fadl to make a surprise attack and capture the ammunition. Selim was in a very precarious position and at first welcomed Emin on the assumption that he was leading another relief expedition from Egypt. When he discovered the truth and was asked to sign on for the German cause, Emin was rebuffed again, only 29 of Selim's men agreeing to follow their ex-governor. This in itself was a further burden on Emin's poorly equipped expedition, as the 29 brought along 153 dependents who would have to be fed and looked after.

In August, the caravan set off to find a route to the Cameroons. It was a disaster, and by November they were back at Selim's camp, only to discover that events had moved fast in their absence and that Selim had gone. Fadl el Mulla had negotiated an agreement with the Mahdists against the wishes of his men, who as a group had mutinied and gone over to Selim Bey. At a stroke, Selim's force had been increased by some 800 troops and thousands of dependents, the feeding and organising of whom presented a major problem. This was solved by another visitor, who appeared on the scene in September. Captain Frederick Lugard had just secured Uganda for Sir William Mackinnon's Imperial British East Africa Company and came to offer Selim Bey the opportunity to take service with the company. Selim and all the forces under his command agreed and marched off to start a new life. They would be joining others from Equatoria in the service of Sir William. Those who had been delivered to Cairo by Stanley did not stay there long. Most of them signed on with the company and were already with Lugard under the command of Shukri Aga, one of Emin's few loyal officers who had accompanied him to the coast.

Fadl hung on in the hills, living the life of a bandit until his luck changed with the appearance of a force from the Congo Free State under Captain van Kerckhoven, who hired him and his men to work for the State. Van Kerckhoven, incidentally, died on this expedition as the result of a shooting accident. King Leopold was the new tenant of Equatoria, having come to an agreement with Sir William to lease the land. At the last, both King Leopold and Sir William Mackinnon got their way. The options delivered by Stanley had been taken up in full.

Shortly after Emin's arrival at Selim's deserted camp, an epidemic of smallpox broke out amongst his followers. Those who were still healthy were sent away and eventually returned to Bukoba, whilst Emin stayed to treat the sick. He remained in the camp for seven months, until the end of May 1892. Then, with a little band of survivors, he decided to make his way to the Congo. By this time, Arab followers of the trader Kilonga-Longa had arrived on the scene. They agreed to escort Emin and his party to the river.

Over the next few months they made their slow and painful way through the forest, marching to the south-west, until in early October they arrived at the village of Chief Kinena. Here they halted to await permission to proceed from the main Arab in the area, Hamadi bin Ali, known as Kibonge, the man who was later to become a partner of Charles Stokes, the arms and ivory dealer hanged by the Belgians. Unfortunately for Emin Pasha, he had stumbled into Kibonge's district at the wrong time. The Free State had just embarked on its war against the Arab slave traders, and Kibonge was in no mood to be helpful. His emissaries, Ismaili and Mamba, returned to Kinena's village on 23 October. The Pasha was expecting a pass allowing him free passage, but what the men carried was his death warrant. After being tricked into separation from his followers, Emin was thrown to the ground and held down while Mamba cut his throat. A futile and pointless end but, perhaps, a fitting conclusion to the bizarre story of Eduard Schnitzer, one-time governor of Equatoria.

Emin had liaisons with at least two women during his time in Africa and was survived by two daughters. The elder, Farida, had accompanied her father on the march to the coast, where she remained when Emin left on his last expedition. She later lived for many years in southern Germany and died of influenza in 1923. The younger daughter was just two, and was with her father when he died. She was taken into the care of the Free State authorities, but there is no record of what became of her.

*****

Henry Morton Stanley, after spending some months in Cairo writing his book of the expedition, *In Darkest Africa*,

returned to Europe to be showered with awards and honours and to face a growing controversy over the conduct of the officers of the Rear Column, in particular that of Major Barttelot and James Jameson. Accusations relating to Barttelot's brutality and eventual insanity and to Jameson's participation in a cannibal feast originated both from the Egyptian interpreter, Assad Farran, who had been dismissed from the expedition, and from William Bonny. Incompetence was added to these charges by Stanley's account of affairs, which blamed the officers for the débâcle of the Rear Column. The dead men's powerful relatives defended their honour, to the delight of the newspapers of the day. Although the two main witnesses were largely discredited, it seemed that the basic charges were true. Certainly, Barttelot's mania for camp discipline was extreme, and Jameson recorded in detail the cannibal incident he witnessed, but in which he took no part. As to the charges of incompetence, it hardly

A stop at Mombasa where Stanley and his officers are greeted by local school-children.

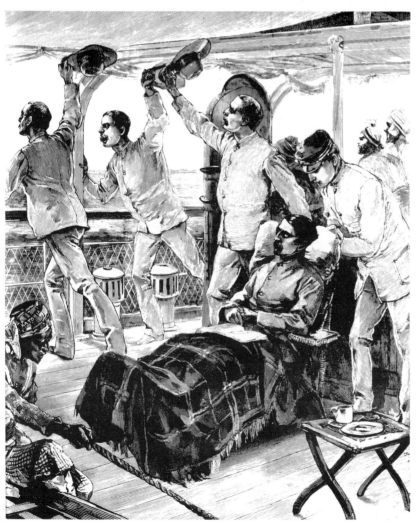

A last hearty farewell to Africa.

matters now, but Stanley's refusal to accept any of the blame himself was less than honest.

These questions had no effect on his huge popularity. The book was an instant best seller, and when he married Dorothy Tennant in Westminster Abbey, shortly after his return to England, an escort of mounted police was needed to clear a route for the couple through the crowds. Africa had taken its toll on his health and throughout the closing years of his life he suffered from recurring bouts of serious illness. He was still the confidant of King Leopold and, through his discussions with the king, was for a long time sure that he would have to return to Congo to impose order on the chaos that had developed there. Partly to avoid this eventuality, his wife persuaded him to stand for Parliament. Against his better judgement, he agreed and on his second attempt was elected, but it did not suit him. A life of all talk and no action was not a recipe to satisfy the great adventurer.

He made one more trip to Africa, to attend the ceremony marking the opening of the railway line from Cape Town to Bulawayo. Whilst in South Africa, he took

the opportunity to meet the Boer leader, President Kruger, and make his own assessment of the gathering storm in that part of the continent. On his return to England, he lectured Parliament on the inevitability of war in South Africa, but few wanted to listen.

In 1899 Stanley was honoured with a knighthood. To many it seemed to have come very late in the day, but he did not renounce his American citizenship until 1892, when he stood for Parliament. In 1900 he retired from politics and took his pleasure in domestic arrangements. The Stanleys had adopted a four-year-old child, Denzil, and moved to a house in the country, Furze Hill in Surrey. These two interests, together with the loving relationship with his wife, brought great comfort to him in his last years. Bouts of sickness were becoming more frequent and his last attack started on 5 May 1904.

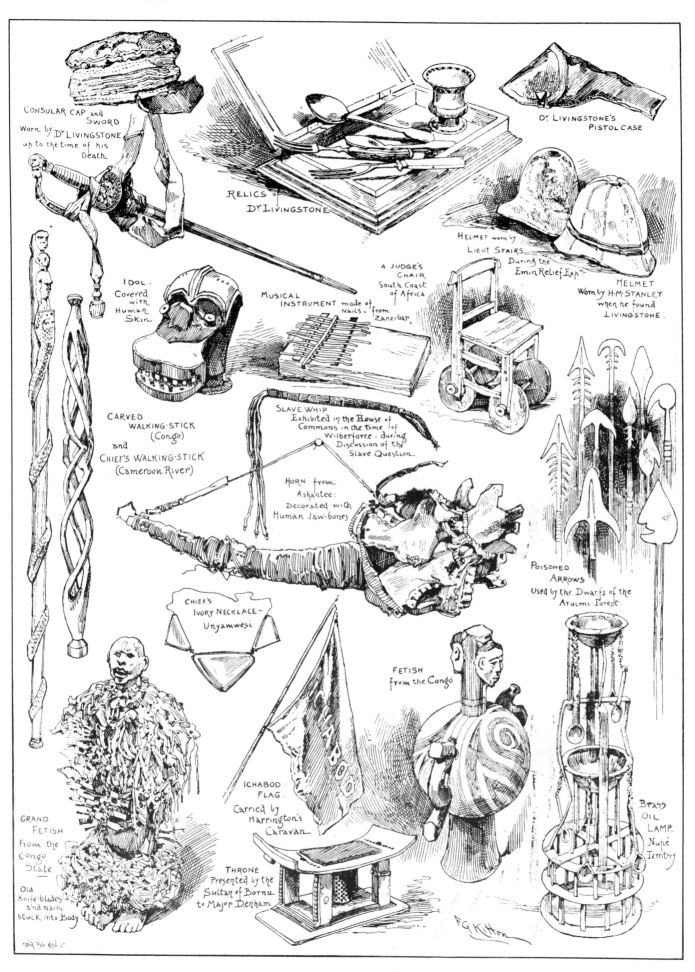

CONSULAR CAP and SWORD Worn by Dr LIVINGSTONE up to the time of his Death

RELICS of Dr LIVINGSTONE

Dr LIVINGSTONE'S PISTOL CASE

HELMET worn by Lieut STAIRS During the Emin Relief Expⁿ

HELMET Worn by H·M·STANLEY when he found LIVINGSTONE.

IDOL. Covered with Human Skin

MUSICAL INSTRUMENT made of Nails - from Zanzibar,

A JUDGE'S CHAIR South Coast of Africa

CARVED WALKING-STICK (Congo) and CHIEF'S WALKING-STICK (Cameroon River)

SLAVE WHIP Exhibited in the House of Commons in the time of Wilberforce - during Discussion of the Slave Question

HORN from Ashantee: Decorated with Human Jaw-bones

POISONED ARROWS Used by the Dwarfs of the Atulmi Forest.

CHIEF'S IVORY NECKLACE - Unyamwesi

FETISH from the Congo

GRAND FETISH from the Congo State Old Knife-blades and Nails stuck into Body

ICHABOD FLAG. Carried by Harrington's Caravan

THRONE Presented by the Sultan of Bornu to Major Denham

BRASS OIL LAMP. Nupé Territory

F.G. Kitton

Stanley was showered with honours. Here he receives the Freedom of the City of London.

The presentation casket that held Stanley's Freedom of the City of London.

He hung on with characteristic tenacity, but eventually died at 6 am on 10 May at the age of 64. The last of the heroic class of explorer had passed away. His like would not be seen again.

During the researches for this book, I came across an early demonstration recording made by Stanley in 1890. His voice came through the crackle of the years strong and firm, confirming the impression he gives of himself in his writings. What was surprising was that it still retained a distinct Welsh lilt. There could be no doubt about his origins. It was a strange, eerie feeling hearing, for the first time, the voice of the man who had existed for us only in musty books and on scraps of paper. It made his existence, at last, very real.

*****

As to the officers of the expedition, few fared as well as Stanley. Barttelot and Jameson had died in the Congo. Captain Nelson was soon back in Africa serving with Mackinnon's Imperial British East Africa Company in Kenya, where he died of dysentery in 1892. Stairs also returned to Africa, but with no better luck. He led an expedition to the south of the Congo for the *Compagnie du Katanga*, dying on the return journey in 1892. The following year, the expedition doctor, Parke, died of a heart attack. Bonny had a hard time when he returned to England, suffering from the twin complaints of poverty and constant illness. Both Stanley and Jephson did what they could for him, but he was to die a bitter man in a poor-house in 1899. Jephson was the one man who remained a close friend of Stanley's to the end. For a time he tried his hand at farming in New Zealand, but never really recovered his health in full after Africa and died in 1908. Troup, after his brief appearance on the world stage, seems to have disappeared from view. Ward reported that he was still alive in 1910, but

more I have not been able to discover. Herbert Ward's story is a happier one. He followed a successful career as an artist and sculptor, drawing heavily on his African experiences for his subjects. On the outbreak of the First World War, he joined the Red Cross and served till 1919, when his health broke and he died at the age of 53.

The last survivor of the Emin Pasha Relief Expedition was Stanley's servant, William Hoffman, who led a very chequered life. At the end of the expedition, he did not return to England, but spent a year on the coast working for the Imperial British East Africa Company out of Mombasa on anti-slavery patrols. Following a brief period in Europe, he then enlisted in the service of the Congo Free State and fought in the campaigns against

Before going their separate ways Parke, Nelson, Stanley, Jephson and Stairs were photographed in Cairo. This engraving was made from the photograph.

Refused his last wish to be laid to rest alongside Livingstone in Westminster Abbey, Stanley was buried in a country graveyard near his home at Pirbright in Surrey. His wife saw to it that the spot was marked by a suitably heroic rugged stone.

the Arabs in the eastern Congo. He claimed to have presided over the court martial and execution of six Arabs implicated in the murder of Emin Pasha. On returning to England, he managed a group of pygmies, who toured the music halls giving demonstrations of their music and dancing. He kept in touch with Stanley and accompanied him on his last trip to Africa for the opening of the Bulawayo railway. He popped up again with the publication of a book on the Emin Pasha expedition in 1938, but further than that I have been unable to discover his fate.

Lastly, I come to the slave trader Tippu Tip. After his return to Zanzibar, he lost his African empire but was left sufficient money to live out a comfortable retirement on the island, writing his autobiography and outliving Stanley by just one year. He died in 1905.

Bibliography

ANSTEY, R. *I Presume: H.M. Stanley's Triumph and Disaster.* (London, 1956).

BARTTELOT, W.G. *The Life of Edmund Musgrave Barttelot.* (Richard Bentley, London, 1890).

CASATI, G. *Ten Years in Equatoria and the return with Emin Pasha.* (Warne, London, 1891).

CONRAD, J. *Heart of Darkness.* (London, 1902).

FORBATH, P. *The Congo River.* (Secker & Warburg, London, 1978).

GOULD, T. *In Limbo.* (Hamish Hamilton, London, 1979).

HARMAN, N. *Bwana Stokesi.* (Cape, London, 1986).

HAWKER, G. *The Life of George Grenfell.* (Religious Tract Society, London, 1909).

HOFFMAN, Wm. *With Stanley in Africa.* (Cassell, London, 1938).

JAMESON, J.S. *The Story of the Rear Column of the Emin Relief Expedition.* (Pater, London, 1890).

JEAL, T. *Livingstone.* (Heinemann, London, 1973).

JEPHSON, A.J.M. *Emin Pasha and the Rebellion at the Equator.* (Samson Low, London, 1890).

JONES, R. *The Rescue of Emin Pasha.* (Alison & Busby London, 1972).

KELTIE, J.S. *The Story of Emin's Rescue.* (Harper, New York, 1890).

MANNING, O. *The Remarkable Expedition.* (Heinemann, London, 1947).

MAURICE, A. *Stanley: Lettres Inédites.* (Office de Publicité, Brussels, 1955).

MIDDLETON, D. *The Diary of A.J. Mounteney Jephson.* (Hakluyt Society, Cambridge, 1969).

MOOREHEAD, A. *The White Nile.* (Hamish Hamilton, London, 1960).

PARKE, T.H. *My Personal Experiences in Equatorial Africa.* (Samson Low, London, 1891).

SMITH, I.R. *The Emin Pasha Relief Expedition.* (Oxford University Press, Oxford, 1972).

STANLEY. Lady D. *The Autobiography of H.M. Stanley.* (Samson Low, London, 1909).

STANLEY, H.M. *How I Found Livingstone.* (Samson Low, London, 1872). *Through the Dark Continent.* (Samson Low, London, 1879). *In Darkest Africa.* (Samson Low, London, 1890).

STANLEY, R./NEAME, A. *The Exploration Diaries of H.M. Stanley.* (Wm. Kimber, London, 1962).

STIGAND, C.H. *Equatoria The Lado Enclave.* (Constable, London, 1923).

TROUP, J.R. *With Stanley's Rear Column.* (Chapman & Hall, London, 1890).

WARD, H. *My Life with Stanley's Rear Column.* (Chatto & Windus, London, 1891). *A Voice from the Congo.* (Heinemann, London, 1910).

WASSERMANN, J. *H.M. Stanley Explorer.* (Cassell, London, 1932).

WEST, R. *Brazza of the Congo.* (Cape, London, 1972).

WHITELY, W.H. Maisha ya Hamed Bin Muhammed El Murjebi yaani *Tippu Tip* [Autobiography Translation]. (East African Literature Bureau, 1966).

Index

Page numbers in italics refer to illustrations.

174